Jan. 1988

Hope you enjoy this!
     Love
        Lynne, Ian and Nicholas

The
BOOK
OF
GOLF
DISASTERS
&
BIZARRE
RECORDS

Also available

The Book of Rugby Disasters and Bizarre Records

Fran Cotton

The Cricketer Book of Cricket Disasters and Bizarre Records

Christopher Martin-Jenkins

Bedside Darts

Sid Waddell

The
BOOK
OF
GOLF
DISASTERS
&
BIZARRE
RECORDS

Chris Plumridge

Introduction by
Terry Wogan

Illustrations by
David Haldane

Stanley Paul
London Melbourne Sydney Auckland Johannesburg

Stanley Paul & Co. Ltd
An imprint of Century-Hutchinson Ltd
17-21 Conway Street, London W1P 6 JD

Hutchinson Group (Australia) Pty Ltd
16-22 Church Street, Hawthorn, Melbourne, Victoria 3122

Hutchinson Group (NZ) Ltd
32-34 View Road, PO Box 40-086, Glenfield, Auckland 10

Hutchinson Group (SA) Pty Ltd
PO Box 337, Bergvlei 2012, South Africa

First published 1985

Set in Century Schoolbook

Made by Lennard Books
Mackerye End, Harpenden
Herts AL5 5DR

Editor Michael Leitch
Designed by David Pocknell's Company Ltd
Production Reynolds Clark Associates Ltd

British Library Cataloguing in Publication Data
Golf disasters
1. Golf-Anecdotes, facetiae, satire, etc.
I. Plumridge, Christopher
796.352'0207 GV967

ISBN 0 09 162870 9

Printed and bound in Spain by
TONSA, San Sebastian

CONTENTS

Introduction 7
Golf: A Pilgrim's Progress 10
Bizarre Championship Records 12
Normal Service Will Be Resumed As Soon As Possible 20
Great Scoring Disasters 26
Bizarre Match-Play Records 32
Technical Hitches 38
International Incidents 44
Grievous Bodily Golf: A Bizarre Record 50
The Simple Act Of Putting 54
Famous Horror Holes 60
Animal Crackers 66
Bizarre Sudden-Death Records 70
Dramatic Turnarounds 72
Feminine Frailty 78
Bizarre Feats And Superior Records 84
Get Me To The Tee On Time 88
Bizarre Strokes 92
Wartime Golf 100
Shots Heard Around The World 106
The Most Violent Game 110
Aces High And Low 116
Acknowledgments 121

INTRODUCTION

I see that the author has taken his courage, his ribbed-faced mashie-niblick and his future happiness in both hands, and, probably without even checking if his right hand was too far over, dedicated this somewhat eccentric tome to someone other than his wife! I'm sure that, at the time, it must have seemed like a droll idea; I'm equally certain that he had a mental picture of the good woman smiling contentedly at the quaint notion, as she busied herself ironing his wood-covers.

By now, of course, he has learned the error of his ways, and is reduced to ironing his own wood-covers and probably even cleaning his own golf shoes! I see that you recoil in shock and horror – surely no wife worthy of the name would reduce her man to such indignity? Ha! I see you know little of the woman scorned, the golf-widow rejected. It's as if the man had hit the lady behind the ear with a putting-iron . . .

This, lest we forget, is The Woman Who Gave Up Everything for a golfing fiend who can't even remember to keep his head still . . . This is the same, selfless, sainted person who Sits at Home Twiddling Her Thumbs All Evening With Nobody But The Children To Talk To Until You Decide To Come Home From The Golf Club . . .

And he hasn't even taken the minor precaution of dedicating the book to her! Nor need he look for comfort and succour from his family. A quick perusal will readily show that he's given his two daughters the elbow, into the bargain. Where does he propose to go for his Christmas dinner when he's old and grey? Whose grandchildren does he imagine he's going to dandle on his knee? Who does he think will be around on visitor's day at the Home?

Can he count on 'golf's countless also-rans', to whom he *has* dedicated this slim volume? Some hopes. There's no such animal. It shows culpable, not to say dangerous ignorance of the psychological make-up of his fellow-golfers to assume that a man is an 'also-ran' just because he six-putts from four feet, or shanks nine times in a row. I've seen Lee Trevino and Hale Irwin miss

'em from six inches, Tom Watson take four to get out of a bunker, and every golfer knows that a shank is only a whisker away from being a good shot ...

You will never meet the man who admits to being a bad golfer, any more than you will meet one who admits to being a bad driver, a lousy lover, or unable to hold his drink ...

Golfers with high handicaps – that's anyone over 16, yes, I am 16 (at Temple GC, since you ask) – are not *bad* golfers, and *certainly* not, as your author would have it, 'also-rans'. Nor are they 'chickens', 'rabbits', 'bunglers' or 'wreckers'. They are 'golfers'. And there are only golfers! Certainly, I will freely admit that there are golfers better than me. They practise more. They do it for a living. They're out on the course all day, to the detriment of their wife, family, career and dog.

A doctor friend of mine recently went skiing for the first time, and took dog's abuse from the instructor, till flesh and blood could take no more. Goaded beyond endurance, the otherwise placid medico turned on his tormentor and shrieked: 'Look, you. *You* can ski, and *I* can't! But can *you* take out an appendix?' The effect, apparently, was somewhat vitiated by the good doctor falling over in the snow as he made his point; but we golfers know what he meant.

Heavens! If I only had the time to play twice and three times a week, like some of these Johnnies, I could be down to single figures in *no* time! Don't talk to me about Seve Ballesteros! He's been playing since he was a child. When you and I were conjugating Latin verbs, he was out there, practising chip shots! Tom Watson? Ben Crenshaw? Don't make me laugh! What couldn't *we* have done, with a golf scholarship to the University of Houston?

'Also-rans'? Bread-winners, rather, toiling at the workface. Men and women who, if only they had been given a chance, if only they had the time, if only ... if only ...

You know, it would serve this bandit right if his wife took up the game. And, in six months, became a better golfer than him. I know, I *was* the caddie ...

GOLF:

A

PILGRIM'S

PROGRESS

Golf is a game of paradox. If we want the ball to fly to the right, we have to aim left; if we want the ball to fly to the left, we have to aim right; to make the ball fly up, we have to hit down; to make it fly low, we have to hit up. It is rather like rubbing your head and your stomach in opposite directions at the same time. Few of us ever master it and, even if we do, we know our new-found aptitude can depart as abruptly as it arrived.

It is these moments of uncoordinated chaos that this book explores. It delves into the reasons why bodies become disconnected from brains, and men and women are overcome by a kind of madness and commit acts of unparalleled horror. In short, it's all about the tragedy, grief, woe and crisis which culminate in disaster on the golf course.

I have always felt that golf is a little like the image of the True Good Life of the Spirit, a microcosm of man's travail and aspirations. All golfers experience their own particular Slough of Despond but, in so doing, do they not also become better for it? In the search for perfection, which is secretly acknowledged as unattainable, are not the trees, bunkers and water hazards put there to test our strength of will so that, at the end, we emerge stronger in spirit and tempered by our misfortune?

In compiling this book I quickly learned to develop a dispassionate attitude to the myriad horrors presented to me. In a way, it was comforting to discover that whatever disaster had befallen me on the links, there was always somebody else who had fared a great deal worse. Apart from six-putting from four feet on one occasion and circumnavigating a green with nine successive shanks on another, my own most memorable disaster can only be judged according to which part of the political spectrum you happen to favour. At Trevose in Cornwall I nearly brained Denis Thatcher with a hooked iron shot

Overcoming disaster at an early age, Chris Plumridge in action at Sunningdale in 1961.

while playing behind him. People with certain political views will consider it a disaster that I missed, while others will think it a disaster that I am not doing extensive porridge in one of Her Majesty's lock-ups.

As far as the bizarre records in this book are concerned, they make no claim to be definitive. Indeed, as millions of golf shots are struck every year, it is quite likely that many of the records have been broken even as you read this. Also, many of the stories have no doubt been embellished as they have passed through the folklore of the game and while every attempt has been made to establish authenticity, poetic licence may be claimed in certain areas. Above all, this is intended to be a light-hearted book which seems appropriate since without a sense of humour, golfers would populate and dominate most of the mental institutions in the world.

Finally, I pondered long and hard over the candidate to whom this book should be dedicated. Naturally, my initial selection was my wife Vanessa, whose support and enthusiasm for the task was unflagging but who would, I felt, not take kindly to adorning a book about disasters and bizarre records. My two daughters were also considered but paternal pride rejected them for the same reasons. Then it came to me in a flash of inspiration. Someone once said that nobody remembers who finished second.

It is to golf's countless also-rans that this book is dedicated.

Chris Plumridge

BIZARRE
CHAMPIONSHIP
RECORDS

MOST NOTORIOUS COLLAPSE

As befits the orderly structure of golf, the game's glittering prizes are neatly categorized into four major championships. They are the Open Championship, often referred to as the British Open, the United States Masters, the United States Open and the United States Professional Golfers' Association Championship. These championships are the big ones, the titles every golfer dreams of winning. A man may win the Paducah Classic ten years in a row and millions in prize-money, but unless he captures one of the big titles, his career will remain incomplete.

       The final hole of the 1939 US Open at Spring Mill, Philadelphia was the site of the most notorious collapse in a major championship. The victim was Sam Snead, still a relative freshman in professional golf, but whose emerging talent was very much evident. Arriving on that fateful 72nd tee, Snead had to wait nearly half an hour before he could drive. In those days, communications were a haphazard affair and Snead had no real idea what was required of him on the par-five hole. In fact, the best score in was 284 which meant that he could afford the luxury of a six and still tie.

His drive finished on the edge of the rough on a bare lie but, believing he needed a birdie four to win, Snead gambled on going for the green with his second shot. Using a brassie, he caught the ball thin, sending it into a bunker where it buried. Still seeking his birdie, Snead tried to reach the green from the sand but the ball stuck in between some freshly laid turfs along the lip. Another hack followed, this time sending the ball into another bunker further on. Having expended four strokes, Snead was then informed that he needed to get down in two more to tie the lead. He made a noble effort, getting the ball onto the green and just missing a long putt for the tie. The fact that he needed two more shots is somehow irrelevant: he had already done enough. That infamous eight was forever scarred on his golfing soul and although he won all the other three major titles, the US Open was the one big one which eluded him.

MOST INFECTIOUS FAILURE

The 18th at Royal Lytham & St Annes provides the most daunting final tee shot in British championship golf. From the tee, a necklace of bunkers runs away diagonally to the right, ending by a clump of bushes. Further on, running up the left side of the fairway are three more bunkers waiting to catch the pulled drive. When a par four is required to win the Open Championship, the landing area for the drive shrinks to minute proportions in the mind of the challenger. In the 1958 Open, three players, Eric Brown, Christy O'Connor and Leopoldo Ruiz all came to the 72nd tee needing a par to tie. In a lemming-like display, all three of them saw their drives plunge into sand. Brown and O'Connor both took five while Ruiz finished with seven.

Disaster at the prize-giving of the 1983 Open Championship. Tom Watson holds together the trophy which he had earlier dropped.

BIGGEST MIGHT-HAVE-BEEN

Even in the first round of a championship, events can conspire to let a player know that, however well he is playing, his attempt is futile. When Tony Jacklin arrived at St Andrews for the 1970 Open, having won the US Open a month earlier, most pundits felt he would be too emotionally drained to put up a good show. In fact, Jacklin was still on an emotional 'high' and began his first round by taking the Old Course apart. When he chipped in for a two at the 9th, he was out in 29, seven under par.

As he turned for home, a bank of ominous black clouds gathered on the horizon and by the time he reached the 14th, the rain was lashing down. As he swung into his second shot on the 14th, an unknown voice shouted 'Fore', causing Jacklin to jump involuntarily at the shot; the ball flew off to the right and landed in a bush. Moments later play was suspended and when it resumed the following day, the mood had departed Jacklin. He took six at the 14th and finished with a round of 67, an excellent score by any account but we shall never know what it might have been.

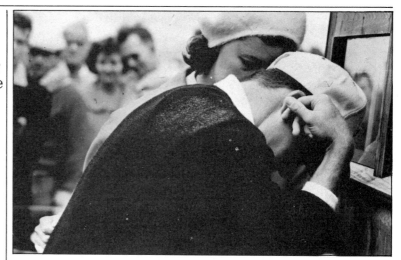

The agony of a final-hole 6 at the 1959 Open Championship at Muirfield for Gary Player and his wife.

BIGGEST HEART-BREAKER

Tony Jacklin was the victim of the supernatural wizardry of Lee Trevino in the 1972 Open at Muirfield. Playing with the American in the third round, Jacklin had to watch as Trevino birdied the final five holes for a round of 66, holing a bunker shot and chip in the process. Jacklin's own 67 was a stupendous effort in the face of these dramatics and left him one behind. In the final round, the two were paired together again and eventually arrived at the 17th tied for the lead. It was Trevino who cracked, pulling his drive into a pot bunker and, after hacking out and hitting his third shot, he still lay behind Jacklin's two solid blows towards this long par-five hole. Trevino's fourth shot skipped through the green to finish at the foot of a grassy bank and then Jacklin played a careful chip some fifteen feet short of the hole. Then Trevino delivered his most decisive piece of sleight of hand.

Having virtually conceded the championship to Jacklin, he took a casual swipe at his ball and watched in amazement as it flopped onto the green and trickled into the hole. This was more than any man could take and Jacklin, in an effort to hole his putt, ran it four feet past and then missed the return. Now a stroke ahead, Trevino played the last hole like a champion while Jacklin played it in a daze for a five. The wound inflicted on that July day never really healed and marked the gradual decline of Jacklin as a force in major championships.

MOST UP-AND-DOWN FINISHER

Just as Arnold Palmer's aggressive style of play enabled him to win tournaments from seemingly impossible positions, so, without this stimulus, he was subject to disastrous collapses. In fact, complacency was Palmer's biggest enemy on the golf course and when his superlative play put him far ahead of the field, that was when he was at his most vulnerable. In the 1961 US Masters Palmer came to the final hole needing a par four for victory over Gary Player. His drive was perfect, leaving him just a seven-iron to the green. As he walked up the fairway he graciously accepted the congratulations of the crowd who felt, as he did, that it was all over and he would become the first man, at that time, successfully to defend the title.

The seeds of complacency thus sown, Palmer settled down to the approach shot. The shot was struck with a slightly open face and the ball plummeted into a right-hand greenside bunker. Nothing too disastrous – for all he had to do was splash out and, at worst, two putts would tie him with Player. The resultant bunker shot was not a splash, it was one of those which makes that ominous sound of ball on metal, meaning that the ball has been hit without too much sand and, in Palmer's case, it sent the ball flying over the other side of the green. Now he was sweating. He had to get down in two more to tie. He putted from a long way off the green and sent the ball 15 feet past the hole. His return effort touched the rim of the cup but span out. He finished in a tie for second place.

Five years later in the 1966 US Open at the Olympic Club, San Francisco, Palmer lay seven strokes ahead of his nearest challenger, Billy Casper, with whom he was also playing, with just nine holes to play. There was little left to stimulate Palmer, except perhaps the chance to beat the existing 72-hole aggregate record set by Ben Hogan in 1948. Beating records never provided the right sort of motivation for Palmer, however, who liked to beat people. Searching in his subconscious for a challenge, Palmer found none, and while he was brooding on this, Casper was producing birdies to Palmer's bogeys. The old complacency factor overtook Palmer on those final nine holes and he ditched the seven strokes to finish in a tie with Casper. In the play-off, Palmer was still in shock from the previous day's events and lost by four strokes.

MOST SLIPSHOD PERFORMANCES

Some not-so-nifty footwork cost two players the chance of victory in a couple of third-round calamities. In the 1921 Open at St Andrews, the English amateur Roger Wethered trod on his ball while walking backwards from the hole and was penalized by one stroke. Inevitably, he finished in a tie for the title and, equally inevitably, lost the play-off.

In the 1946 US Open at Canterbury Country Club, Ohio, Byron Nelson's caddie put the boot in when he accidentally kicked his master's ball on the 16th green. The single penalty stroke incurred put Nelson in a play-off with Lloyd Mangrum which the latter won.

MOST SHATTERING EXPERIENCE

While dramatic events in major championships tend to be condensed into the final few holes, incidents do occur in earlier rounds that, with hindsight, have a profound effect on the result. The best-known example concerned Harry Bradshaw and the infamous broken bottle in the 1949 Open at Royal St George's. Bradshaw had begun his championship challenge with a pretty 68 to lead the field, and when he started his second round the larks were singing and the sun was glinting on the waters of Pegwell Bay. On the 5th hole, the joy evaporated. From his drive, Bradshaw's ball came to rest in the remains of a broken beer bottle. Unsure of his rights, he elected to play the ball and, taking his wedge, smashed both ball and bottle up the fairway. He took six on the hole and, his concentration disrupted, 77 for the round. He battled on to finish in a tie with Bobby Locke after 72 holes but was buried in the play-off by twelve strokes.

MOST FEEBLE FINISH

Communications were the cause of Argentinian Jose Jurado's failure to win the 1931 Open at Carnoustie. Jurado went into the final round with a four-stroke lead and eventually arrived at the last two holes needing a four-five finish to win or, more realistically considering Carnoustie's rugged 17th and 18th holes, two fives to tie. His drive on the 71st hole avoided the insidious Barry Burn but his four-iron second shot didn't – he topped it into the water and holed out in six. Misinformed about what he had to do, he tamely played the last hole for a five and lost by a single stroke to Tommy Armour.

MOST CHARMING LOSER

Some 10 million people watching the 1968 US Masters on television witnessed Roberto de Vicenzo gain a birdie three on the 17th hole in the final round. One very important person apparently didn't see the birdie, namely Tommy Aaron who was playing with de Vicenzo and marking his card. Aaron put down a four on the Argentinian's card. At the completion of the round, de Vicenzo signed his card for what he thought was a 65 and was rushed off for a TV interview as it was likely he would be the winner or at least tie with Bob Goalby for the title. Suddenly it became clear that a dreadful error had been perpetrated. In signing his card, de Vicenzo had made his four at the 17th inviolate and his total for the round, 66, had to stand in spite of any breast-beating that the rule was stupid, unfair or whatever. Goalby was the Masters champion by one stroke, a hollow victory from which he never recovered. On the other hand, de Vicenzo took this disaster on the chin and in his speech at the prize-giving, remarked in his broken English: 'What a stupid I am.'

MOST CONFIDENT CHAMPION

If ever a player tempted the fates to deliver the sand-filled sock to the base of the skull it was Max Faulkner. Before the start of the final round of the 1951 Open at Royal Portrush, Faulkner was found to be signing autographs as 'The 1951 Open Champion'. His confidence was well-founded – he won by two strokes.

MOST OFFENSIVE STROKE

Having missed the 36-hole cut in the 1979 US Open at Inverness, Ohio, Bobby Clampett, then an amateur, was called out for the third round to act as a marker. On the first tee, Clampett struck his opening drive 220 yards up the middle from a kneeling position. A United States Golf Association official stepped forward and warned that this sort of behaviour could not be tolerated and he was not to repeat it. Clampett ignored the warning and later in the round repeated the kneeling tee shot and compounded the felony by putting between his legs with a wedge. The news of these incidents filtered back and officials rushed to the 12th tee, showed Clampett the red card and ordered him off the course.

Clampett went on to earn his own place in major championship disasters when he led the Open Championship at Royal Troon in 1982 with opening rounds of 67 and 66. His final two rounds were 22 strokes worse and he finished in a tie for tenth place.

FIRST SUDDEN DEATH
(US MASTERS)

After 69 holes of the 1979 US Masters, Ed Sneed stood on the brink of his first major championship victory. Playing with calm composure he had dominated the tournament and now held a three-stroke lead on the field. His momentum was slightly halted with three putts on the precipitous 16th green but no matter, the 17th was a drive and a flick and a four there would allow him the luxury of a five at the last for victory. Sneed's drive to the 17th was long, leaving him that flick with a wedge. The ball covered the flag all the way, pitched on the green but instead of squirming to a halt, bounced down a grassy bank at the back. Three more strokes ensued and now he had to get a par four at the last to win. He didn't. Missing the green with his approach and chipping up to five feet, Sneed saw his opportunity vanish when his putt hung on the edge and failed to drop. He then joined Fuzzy Zoeller and Tom Watson in the first sudden-death play-off in Masters history, and when Zoeller won on the second extra hole, Sneed had the bemused look of a man for whom disaster would now be a constant bed-fellow.

Head in hands, Mrs Doug Sanders reflects the anguish of her husband's missed putt on the 18th green at St Andrews in 1970.

MOST TRAGIC MISS

Most golfers have imagined themselves facing a short putt to win the Open. 'This for the Open,' they say to themselves and then calmly roll the ball into the hole. In reality they would be lucky to strike the ball at all if they ever found themselves in such a position. In the 1970 Open at St Andrews, Doug Sanders put the pressure totally in perspective when he faced a tricky downhill putt of some two feet to win by one stroke from Jack Nicklaus. With the wind tugging at his trousers, Sanders lined up the putt and then at the last minute reached down to clear some microscopic debris from his line. At that moment, one could sense he would not hole the putt and the resultant nervous shove at the ball provided the final confirmation. This terrible miss earned Sanders worldwide sympathy and elevated him into a kind of Victims' Valhalla where only the most seriously wounded can reside.

Hubert Green was similarly afflicted on the final green of the 1978 US Masters when he faced a putt of three feet to tie with Gary Player. Player had come out of the pack with a closing 64 to set a target which had not been matched. Green's second shot to the 18th green left him with that short birdie putt and he too was standing over the ball ready to putt when he was disturbed, in his case by a nearby radio commentator. Green stepped away, tried to collect himself but to no avail – the ball slid off to the right and Player was the champion for the third time in his career.

Augusta agonies afflict Ed Sneed.

NORMAL SERVICE
WILL BE
RESUMED
AS SOON AS
POSSIBLE

TELEVISION

"....AND AS IT TRICKLES ON TO THE GREEN...."

Take 150 acres of golfing terrain, populate it with 150 players, distribute some 35 miles of cable, numerous cameras, technicians and commentators over its acreage and throw in a few satellite transmissions and you have the perfect set-up for the application of **Sod's Law** (If it can possibly go wrong, it will, and even if it can't, it might).

In recent years, televising golf tournaments has become a major growth industry in the game and, considering the potential for cock-ups, the incidence of disaster is reasonably low. However, when Sod's Law is invoked there is no place to hide for the television company as the medium beams the message into millions of homes. Sometimes, the medium doesn't beam the message at all due either to loss of transmission or rigid adherence to schedules. When this happens, many people feel like following the example of the American Walker Cup player watching the closing stages of the 1955 US Open at Olympic. As Jack Fleck stood over his historic final-green putt to tie with Ben Hogan, the television company cut the transmission. This particular viewer was so enraged that he **hurled an ashtray through the screen.**

Similar lack of consideration was demonstrated by ITV in the closing stages of the 1978 European Open at Walton Heath. As Bernard Gallacher came up the last hole needing a four to tie Bobby Wadkins and Gil Morgan, the transmission was cut to make way for a scheduled children's programme. Gallacher got his untransmitted four but lost the play-off while ITV lost the allegiance of millions of viewers. Independent television also made a mess of its transmission of the 1982 US Masters by failing to book enough time on the satellite link. Just as Craig Stadler, the eventual winner, arrived on the last green the picture vanished although the sound remained. The cameras then switched to a **sweating London link-man** who tried manfully to paint a picture of Stadler's subsequent three putts while the American commentary continued. The picture was restored in time to witness Stadler win the play-off against Dan Pohl.

In the 1978 European Open at Walton Heath, ITV instituted on-course interviews during play. On one occasion the interviewer approached Carl Mason with the intention of asking him about the four tough finishing holes he was facing.

'What's the toughest shot you have to play on this closing run?' came the question.

Mason looked at the interviewer rather bleakly. 'The next one,' he replied. 'My ball is lying under that bush.'

Professional Bill Large was playing in a tournament when he felt the urgent call of nature. Repairing to some nearby bushes he was unaware that an overzealous cameraman was recording his progress for national television while the commentator was discussing the 'fluid' swing of his playing companion, Christy O'Connor.

Television equipment does not, as a rule, interfere with the play during a tournament, and even if it does, local rules have been framed to cover most situations such as a ball coming to rest on cables or equipment which interferes with the intended line of a shot. The general rule is that television equipment is regarded as a temporary moveable obstruction, and if a ball strikes it and bounces elsewhere, then the player has to **take it on the chin.** The American Mike Krantz was sucker-punched in this way during the 1980 Scandinavian Open at the Vasatorps course in Sweden. Krantz was leading the tournament after three rounds and was still very much in contention as he arrived at the 16th hole of the final round. Here, his second shot to the green struck the top of a TV camera and bounced out-of-bounds. A distraught Krantz eventually holed out in eight and dropped down to finish in eighth place.

In the 1983 PGA Championship at Royal St George's, Sandy Lyle's ball struck a camera buggy on the 13th hole with the result that the ball bounded away into the rough and was never found. Lyle finished two strokes behind the winner. That was **a bad week for BBC buggies** – one of them accidentally ran over Brian Waites's golf bag and bent his favourite driver.

The all-seeing eye of television played a legal role in the 1980 Tournament of Champions at La Costa, California. The camera picked up Tom Watson on the 13th hole in the process of offering his playing companion, Lee Trevino, some advice. Watson won the tournament by five strokes but this margin was reduced to three as Watson was penalized under Rule 9-la: 'A player may give advice to, or ask for advice from, only his partner or either of their caddies.'

Most viewers believe that, on occasions, they could do a better job of commentating on golf than some of the incumbents. There was certainly room for improvement when Steve Melnyk, a professional golfer employed by CBS Television in America, provided ample proof that professionals should stick to playing golf rather than talking about it. 'Peter Jacobsen,' said Melnyk, 'is in a

Industrial inaction at the 1978 Open Championship caused this ingenious response to the loss of telephone communications.

position where a birdie will help him more than a bogey.' Now, why didn't you think of saying that?

The other medium which gets the message across from golf tournaments is the written word. Golf writers are a dedicated band of professionals, kind to old ladies, children and cats – upright citizens working in fraternal harmony, sometimes in conditions of appalling privation but who all adhere to the first principle of journalism that **the news must get through.**

This latter requirement has produced enough moments of tragedy, farce and pure knockabout comedy to warrant a separate book on the subject, so we shall have to restrict ourselves to a few illuminating examples.

You may recall the story of the Scottish District Nurse at the 1975 Walker Cup at St Andrews who drove her car into a bunker (see 'Feminine Frailty'). Well, she or one of her colleagues was also present at the 1977 Martini International at Blairgowrie. As Greg Norman sank his winning putt, this District Nurse decided to make a quick getaway from the scene and beat the traffic. As she carefully manoeuvred her car round the corner of the press tent, the car bumper hooked up the telephone cables protruding from under the canvas. On she drove, oblivious to the fact that behind her trailed several yards of vital links to the outside world; inside the tent this severance of communications had produced a **condition of mass hysteria.** Tempers were not improved by the writers having to leave the tent en masse and seek out some of the rare telephone boxes in that part of Scotland. But they did, and the news got through.

Reporting from Continental tournaments can produce experiences akin to waiting for Directory Enquiries to answer a request for a number in Vladivostok. At a recent Italian Open, the organizers had arranged telephone cubicles for the press, complete with hot and cold running water. The telephones were located in the shower cubicles of the ladies' locker-room. The resultant reverberations produced by several journalists all shouting their stories back to Fleet Street caused a deputation to complain to the organizers. With typical Latin ingenuity the problem was solved. The next day the shower cubicles were festooned with towels to deaden the noise.

At the same tournament a **bout of kleptomania** swept through the press tent and writers found their belongings disappearing with monotonous regularity. As another item went missing, Renton Laidlaw, the estimable Secretary of the Association of Golf Writers, flung off his raincoat and stormed up to an official, demanding that something be done about the lamentable security. When he had finished his tirade, he turned round to collect his coat. It too had been stolen.

Moments of humour during post-round interviews with players are rare. Carefully phrased questions from the press are usually answered with a carefully guarded reply of 'Yup' or 'Nope'. One memorable moment did occur,

Above: Carnage at the 1961 Open Championship at Royal Birkdale.
Below: More devastation at Turnberry during the John Player Golf Classic in 1973.

however, at the 1978 Open Championship when, as the 36-hole leader, Japan's Isao Aoki was brought into the press centre for the customary interview. With the aid of an interpreter and in his own limited English, Aoki described how he 'flee-putted the flifth flom florty fleet' and other similar dramas. As the interview began to flag a little George Simms, the press officer, mentioned to Aoki that he had been in the rough a few times and, to emphasize this, pointed to the floor. Aoki looked puzzled so George, once again, talked about the rough and waved his hand at the floor. At last comprehension dawned on Aoki's face.

'Yes,' he said, 'velly nice carpet.'

The most important thing a golf commentator has to remember is to comment on what is shown on the monitor screen in the commentary box and refrain from commenting on what can be seen on the course outside. During one of the Colgate Ladies tournaments at Sunningdale, BBC commentator Alex Hay **forgot this golden rule.** The commentary box was located near the landing area of the drive on the 17th hole and he could see the US professional Marlene Floyd through the window. He decided to remark of the aesthetic qualities of the 17th and turning to Henry Cotton, also in the commentary box at the time, said:

'This is a beautiful little hole, don't you think, Henry?'

'Yes,' replied Cotton, 'but it was a lot tighter in my day.'

What neither of them realized was that during this exchange of remarks the picture being beamed out into millions of homes showed the delectable Miss Floyd's backside filling the screen as she bent down to examine the lie of her ball.

GREAT
SCORING
DISASTERS

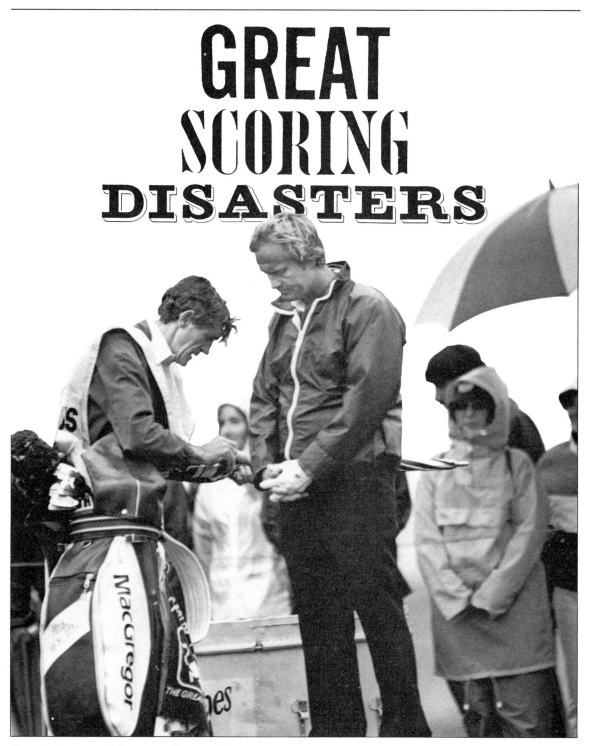

'I make it we need three pars for an 83.'
Jimmy Dickinson appraises Jack Nicklaus of his position in the first round of the 1981 Open Championship.

Most golfers are only too familiar with big numbers. While a string of sevens, eights and nines may not look pretty on a card, the average player can take consolation from the fact that such scores are not the sole preserve of the humble hacker. Admittedly, the world record for the highest score on a single hole is held by a lady amateur (see 'Feminine Frailty') but disasters of such magnificent proportions are relative to each player's ability.

If a modest club player went round Royal St George's in 83 strokes on a cold, wet and windy day he would probably be delighted. However, if Jack Nicklaus produced the same score in the same conditions it would make national headlines. Which is exactly what it did do in the 1981 Open Championship when the great man put together a run of fives and sixes over the Kentish links to record his **highest score in twenty Open attempts.** Nicklaus comfortably beat his previous record of 80 which he set in the 1962 Open at Troon but, to be fair, this score contained a ten at the 11th whereas his Sandwich effort was free of such inconsistencies. Indeed, throughout his long career, Nicklaus has been comparatively unscathed by single-hole disasters.

Another star name who fell victim to the bad-run syndrome was Jerry Pate. Pate came to the 1976 Open Championship at Royal Birkdale having just won the US Open title, clinching his victory with a sublime second shot to the final hole (see 'Shots Heard Around the World'). From that sublimity, Pate went to the ridiculous in the third round at Royal Birkdale, taking 87 strokes to go round but **without hitting double figures on a single hole.**

Double figures of a technical nature were recorded by Australian professional Kel Nagle in the 1969 Alcan tournament. Nagle reached the turn in 34 strokes, a total which his marker inadvertently entered against his score for the 9th hole. At the end of the round, Nagle blithely signed his card only to discover later that his **total for the round was 105.**

As mentioned previously, no one has come close to the 166 strokes taken by the anonymous lady amateur on one hole although a spirited attempt on this record took place in 1984 at Lahinch in Ireland, when another anonymous lady played the short third in 34 strokes. In racking up this score, she set a record of her own for **most strokes taken in a bunker.** Her tee shot landed in the sand and the ball stubbornly refused to reappear on grass until it had been struck another 30 times.

Compared with this, the record for the **highest one-hole score by a professional** seems hardly worth mentioning, standing as it does at a paltry 23 strokes. This record was set by Tommy Armour on the 17th hole in the 1927 Shawnee Open when he deposited ten drives out-of-bounds. Rumour has it that he actually holed out in 21 but, not wishing to suffer disqualification for signing an incorrect scorecard, he preempted any queries concerning the accuracy of his score by stating that he took 23.

Armour's record has stood ever since, although it looked in jeopardy in the 1978 French Open at La Baule when the young French professional Philippe Porquier was suddenly overcome by a fit of the 'Lucy Lockits' (sockets). With his ball resting just fifty yards short of a long par-five hole after two blows, Philippe produced a series of shanks over a boundary fence en route to setting the PGA European Tour record of 21. This score actually tied the record set by a competitor in the 1860 Open Championship, but allowances must be made in this case for condition of the course, equipment available, etc., whereas Porquier's effort was achieved with the full might of technological development at his side.

In 1938, another attempt on Armour's record had been made by Ray Ainsley in the US Open at Cherry Hills. Ainsley's approach shot to the 16th green landed in a fast-flowing brook and the rule about playing the ball as it lies was simply not applicable. The ball would not lie still so Ainsley played it when it came temporarily to rest. Several sodden strokes later he nailed it, the ball erupting from the depths and finishing in a clump of bushes. Once on dry land, he was more in control of his swing but he still came up short of Armour's record, eventually holing out in a modest 19 strokes. His only consolation was that he set the **US Open record for the highest score on a single hole.**

While the efforts of Walter Danecki and Maurice Flitcroft in the Open Championship have been fully recorded elsewhere (see 'Bizarre Feats and Superior Records'), it is interesting to speculate on what might have been in the case of an unnamed Scottish professional playing in the 1935 Open at Muirfield. This particular worthy began his challenge with 7, 10, 5, 10 but then rallied to reach the turn in 65. A chance for permanent enshrinement in the record books looked very much on the cards when he took another ten at the 11th, but on the next hole he took the **coward's way out by retiring** after four unsuccessful attempts to extract his ball from a bunker.

Dropping down the numerical scale, we are assailed by a host of 14s, 13s, 12s and 11s perpetrated by players who make their living from twos, threes and fours. For Australia's Greg Norman, the 17th hole at Lindrick in the 1982

Martini International was just another 397-yard hole which devoured could be with a drive and a pitch. Prior to his drive, Norman was accosted by an inexperienced photographer who wanted an action shot. Nothing doing, said Norman, it would have to wait until the end of the round. The photographer was not so easily put off and, as Norman reached the top of his backswing on the tee shot, his reflexes were sudddenly jolted by the click of a shutter exposing film. The ball swung violently away into some luxuriant undergrowth on fairway. Numerous the left of the hacks and drops under penalty followed before Norman's ball emerged back on the fairway; he eventually holed out in 14.

When Arnold Palmer came to the 9th hole at Rancho Park in the 1961 Los Angeles Open he was handily placed for a good score. The hole was in fact Palmer's finishing hole, so where better to end the day's work with a birdie. The only caveat on the hole concerned the narrow landing area for the drive which was flanked by out-of-bounds. Palmer heeded this and dropped down to a 3-wood. The ball went out-of-bounds on the right. The birdie was now out of the window but he might snatch a five with his next ball. That game plan went by the board when his next attempt went out-of-bounds on the left. Down went another ball, swish went the 3-wood and crack went the ball over the right-hand boundary fence. With an eye for symmetry, he sent his fourth ball over the left-hand fence. His fifth ball found the fairway and visitors to the 9th hole at Rancho Park can now **gaze at a commemorative plaque** which records the day Arnold Palmer completed the hole in 12 strokes.

Almost as impressive was Ben Crenshaw's attack on the 14th hole of the Harbour Town Links in the 1982 Heritage Classic. On a blustery final day, Crenshaw was holding his game together admirably when he came to the 14th, a cunningly constructed par three protected by a lake which runs the length of the hole and to the right of the green. At 152 yards, the hole is no more than a 7-iron, but with a strong wind swooping through the trees, Crenshaw felt that a punched 4-iron was the shot to keep the ball low. The shot was almost perfect, its only imperfection being that it was a couple of yards short. Crenshaw reloaded and tried again, with the same watery result. Convinced he was on the right track, Crenshaw punched another ball. Same result. After the fourth attempt had plunged into the water, Crenshaw began to get an inkling that perhaps his assessment of the shot had been incorrect so he switched to a 3-iron and sent the ball soaring over the back of the green. From there he got down in eleven. He then took eight at the next hole before, as he said afterwards: 'I pulled myself together and finished with three straight bogies.'

Finally, here is a warning to all those golfers who tempt providence in

Lee Trevino behind bars.

the mistaken belief that nothing quite so bad can ever happen to them on a golf course. The year is 1974 and the European Tour has assembled at La Manga for the Spanish Open. The night before the first round, a group of players are sitting around discussing the incidence of high scores. Among their number is one Severiano Ballesteros, then a callow youth of 17. As the discussion developed, Ballesteros snorted that **in his opinion it was impossible** for a professional golfer to score double figures on one hole. The rest of the group shrank back from this obvious heresy, realizing the retribution for such a remark.

The following day, Ballesteros came to the 9th hole, a par five of 586 yards. He hooked his first drive out-of-bounds and then sliced his next ball out-of-bounds. His next effort found the fairway and he was now lying five. His sixth shot finished in a lake so he dropped out for a one stroke penalty. The next shot found a bunker and he eventually made the green in nine. Two putts later the man who said it was impossible completed the hole in 11 strokes.

Seve the Freemason?

BIZARRE
MATCH - PLAY
RECORDS

MOST CRUSHING DEFEATS

'Match-play's the thing,' said Freddie Tait, British Amateur Champion in 1896 and 1898, 'stroke-play's no more than rifle-shooting.' Most golfers would agree that match-play provides an extra dimension to the game, representing the raw blood and guts of man-to-man combat – or woman-to-woman if you want to be pedantic. As well as providing many nerve-tingling moments and dramatic turnarounds, match-play can also be the scenario for crushing defeat.

There was not much raw blood and guts in the woman-to-woman encounter between Cecil Leitch (despite her Christian name, she was undoubtedly female) and Molly McBride in the final of the 1921 Canadian Ladies'

Championship in Ottawa. Miss Leitch was 14 up at the half-way stage of the 36 holes and went on to win by 17 and 15, losing only one hole in the entire match and winning 18 of the 21 holes played. This is the heaviest defeat inflicted in the final of a national championship.

An even heavier defeat was inflicted in 1928 by Archie Compston on Walter Hagen in a 72-hole challenge match at Moor Park. Compston won 18 and 17 but it was Hagen who went on to win the Open Championship of that year with Compston in third place.

More ignominy occurred in the final of the 1934 British Amateur Championship when local man James Wallace failed to win a hole against the American Lawson Little, and lost by 14 and 13. Another winless performance came in the 1920 British Amateur Championship at Muirfield. In one of the early rounds, Captain Carter from Ireland defeated his American opponent by the maximum possible over 18 holes – 10 and 8. The American, not surprisingly, prefers to remain anonymous.

The heaviest defeat in a European Championship final occurred in the French Ladies' Championship of 1927 at Le Touquet when Mlle de la Chaume beat Mrs Alex Johnston by 15 and 14. In the English Amateur Championship final of 1968 Michael Bonallack, then at the peak of his considerable powers, defeated David Kelley 12 and 11 at Ganton. In the morning Bonallack was round in an approximate 61.

MOST PROFITABLE LOSS

In the 1978 World Match-Play, then sponsored by Colgate, a ludicrous situation developed involving Tom Watson and South African Dale Hayes. The two met in the first round and Watson demolished Hayes by 11 and 9. There was a consolation event for first-round losers which Hayes eventually won, taking prize-money of £10,000 coupled with £1,000 for being a first round loser. Watson lost to Ray Floyd in the next round and received just £2,000 for his efforts. The consolation event was then cancelled for future years. Tom Watson didn't say much.

Obviously Hale Irwin is ahead! The Ryder Cup, 1981.

Exhibition foursome at Finchley, 1932. Left to right: Percy Alliss, A.G. Havers, Keith Dalby, A.J. Lacey.

THE BEST OF WENTWORTH

As far as professional golf is concerned, match-play has become virtually extinct. The demands of television and the unpredictability of the finishes have rendered the format unmarketable in commercial terms. Fortunately, one major match-play event still survives, the World Match-Play Championship, played each autumn at Wentworth. This event has been the scene of some stirring encounters, most notably the 1965 match between Gary Player and Tony Lema (see 'Dramatic Turnarounds'). A similar recovery occurred in the 1982 event in the match between Sandy Lyle and Nick Faldo. The two were not exactly bosom pals (see 'Technical Hitches') and Faldo appeared to have the upper hand when at one stage in the match he was six up. However, Lyle clawed his way back and with seven holes to play, the match was all square. Lyle then went two up with three holes to play and won the match by 2 and 1.

In 1972, a few months after the tragic events at Muirfield in the Open Championship (see 'Bizarre Championship Records'), Tony Jacklin found himself facing his old bogeyman, Lee Trevino, for a place in the final. Walking down the first fairway Jacklin, aware of his opponent's capacity for chattering, turned to Trevino and said:

'I'm not talking today.'

Trevino replied: 'You don't have to talk, Tony, just listen.'

At lunch, Jacklin was listening to a four hole deficit but came out like a lion in the afternoon to reach the turn in 29 and square the match. Jacklin was eventually round in 63 but lost on the last green.

MOST IMPREGNABLE VICTOR

At his peak, the legendary Bobby Jones was rarely stretched in a match over 36 holes. In the 1928 Walker Cup, playing in the top singles, Jones defeated Britain's Phil Perkins by 13 and 12. Perkins then had the temerity to battle through to the final of the US Amateur Championship of the same year where he again faced Jones. This time he made more of a fight of it, losing by 10 and 9. (Disaster was a frequent companion in Perkins's life for he settled in America and, during the Prohibition period, became involved in a shoot-out between some gangsters and the police when the gangsters used him as a shield and he was shot in the leg.)

One match in which Jones was extended to the utmost came in the 1930 British Amateur Championship when he faced Britain's Cyril Tolley in an early round over 18 holes. The pair arrived at the 17th, the Road Hole (see 'Famous Horror Holes') all square, then Jones's second shot to the green was alleged to have struck a spectator which prevented the ball from finishing on the road. Other people present swore the ball would have stayed up anyway, but the upshot of it was that Jones halved the hole and went on to win at the 19th. Jones won the Championship and so completed the first leg of his Grand Slam feat, also known as the Impregnable Quadrilateral, of winning the Amateur and Open Championships of both Britain and America in the same year.

MOST DIEHARD LOSER

Only one candidate is offered: Lionel Munn who, in the Amateur Championship of 1908, lost at the 28th. In the same event in 1932 he lost at the 26th and he did so again in 1936, making a total of 26 extra holes without a win.

LONGEST MATCH

In terms of time, the longest match in the history of the World Match-Play Championship occurred in the 1968 semi-final between Tony Jacklin and Gary Player. The two were level after 36 holes and darkness prevented further play that day. The following day it rained continually and no play was possible. Some twenty-four hours later, Jacklin and Player repaired to the first tee for the 37th hole of their encounter. Both men hit the green in two shots and Player holed a nasty putt for his four. Jacklin's putt was slightly shorter and, just as he was standing over the ball, Player turned and remonstrated with the crowd for making too much noise. Whether Player's action was gamesmanship or not we shall never know, but the result was that Jacklin missed his putt and lost.

*Foursomes golf is all about team work! T. Pinner offers constructive advice to his partner
W. Sutherland, having just failed himself to dislodge their ball from the fork of a tree during the 1967
Sunningdale Open Foursomes.*

DISASTER IN TRIPLICATE

The collective anguish of William Greig, Lawrie Auchterlonie and John Ball can easily be understood by any golfer who has dumped his second shot to the first hole at St Andrews into the Swilcan Burn. Each of these three players suffered this fate during the 1895 British Amateur Championship and on each occasion it was the 19th hole. Fate twisted the knife a little further because the sole beneficiary of this trio of disasters was Leslie Balfour-Melville who won his last three matches, including the final, in this way.

UNLUCKIEST BOUNCE

During the last round of the final of the 1912 British Amateur Championship at Westward Ho! between Abe Mitchell and John Ball, Mitchell's tee shot to the short 14th struck an umbrella held up by a spectator and the ball, instead of landing on the green, was diverted into a bunker. Mitchell was leading by two holes at the time but lost the 14th and, subsequently, the match at the 38th.

HIGHEST SCORE TO HALVE A HOLE

In the final of the 1906 British Amateur Championship at Hoylake, J. Robb, the winner, and his opponent, C. Lingen, halved the 6th in nine. Lingen drove out-of-bounds, then played another ball which finished in a bunker. He hit the ball out and put his fifth stroke into another bunker. Meanwhile, his opponent had driven into some bushes, chipped out, put his next in some more bushes, recovered too strongly into a hedge and eventually reached the green in six, the same number as Lingen. Both players then three-putted.

TECHNICAL HITCHES

'There must be some way out of this?' Greg Norman consults the rules during the 1981 Open Championship at Royal St George's.

A golf course is like a battlefield. The obvious emplacements of trees, bunkers and water are clearly defined and the unwary golfing infantry believes that these are the only hazards to avoid. What almost every golfer fails to realize is that just about the whole course is sown with **anti-personnel devices of immense destructive capacity.** These devices are extremely well-hidden but once triggered off they are capable of blowing anybody's score to pieces.

The generals in this particular war game are kindly people, however, and have taken tremendous care to point out the location of these pitfalls and have even gone so far as to recount previous incidents to act as a warning for the future. Despite this attention, thousands of golfers' scores are maimed or wounded every year simply because they do not heed the wise words of the powers-that-be and read the Rules of Golf.

Ignorance of the Rules and their application has probably been responsible for more grief, more tragedy and more heartache than any other aspect of the game. Even the professionals, the men and women who lead us over the top into action, have suffered losses. The following casualty list should act as a memorial tablet to the carnage.

Professional Roger Maltbie arrived at the Manor Country Club in Maryland to try and pre-qualify for the 1984 US Open. In the pro shop, Maltbie was asked if he wanted to rent a golf cart and, since the event was over 36 holes, he thought this would be a desirable way to conserve his energy. After playing nine holes, Maltbie was stopped by an official who asked how long he had been in the buggy. Maltbie replied he had been in and out of the vehicle about six times. Since carts were not allowed, the official slapped a 12-stroke penalty on Maltbie, turning his nine-hole score of 36 into 48. This is the **highest penalty ever imposed on a professional golfer** for actions not involving the striking of the ball. Maltbie decided that his US Open challenge would have to wait another year, and withdrew from the tournament.

In the 1978 Quad Cities Open, US professional Leonard Thompson, one of the game's long-hitters, reached the green at a par-five hole in two shots. He surveyed the eagle putt with care and, having requested his caddie to attend the flagstick, struck a long putt towards the hole. His caddie, seeing a potential improvement in his share of his employer's winnings, went through the set motions as approved by the School of Caddies. He twisted, turned and waved at the ball with his hands in his efforts to influence its path into the hole. Unfortunately, his gyrations caused a tee-peg lodged behind his ear to fall onto the green directly in the path of the ball. The ball struck the tee, diverting it from the hole, and Thompson was penalized two strokes for **striking his own equipment.**

In the play-off for the 1950 US Open at Merion between Lloyd Mangrum, Ben Hogan and George Fazio, Mangrum, on the 16th green, picked up his ball without marking it in order to remove an insect. The action cost him a two-stroke penalty and enabled Hogan to win by four strokes.

In the 1974 French Open at Chantilly, British professional Maurice Bembridge was playing with a Frenchman who, for reasons which will be revealed, shall remain nameless. The Frenchman was accompanied by his grandmother who moved well ahead of him on the fringe of the tree-line which decorates this lovely course. It became increasingly uncanny that every time the Frenchman's ball went into the woods, which was often, it would emerge back on the fairway, closely followed by *grand-mère*. The subterfuge couldn't last and eventually the old lady made her fatal error. On one hole Bembridge noticed that the Frenchman drove off with a black numbered ball which flew into the woods and then reappeared on the fairway bearing red numerals. Bembridge's French was sufficient for him to make the following observation:

'Non, Monsieur, noir dans les arbres, rouge dans le fairway.'
The Frenchman withdrew from the tournament.

American professional Lawson Little was partnering an amateur in a Calcutta Sweepstake event, a form of golf gambling which is now frowned upon by the ruling bodies. The pot in this case was worth $40,000, and as Little and his partner arrived on the final green the amateur needed two putts from a short distance to win all the greenbacks. The amateur putted up to the edge of the hole but, used to having short putts conceded, unconsciously **raked the ball back to have another go.** Little did not shoot himself, or the amateur.

Probably the most common infringement of the Rules committed by professionals is the signing of an incorrect scorecard. As an example of how a jumble of figures can sometimes numb the brain, the case of Severiano Ballesteros in the 1983 Silk Cut Masters tournament at St Pierre springs to mind. At the end of his final round, Ballesteros signed his card which showed his score for the 2nd and 3rd holes as 3-2. In fact he had scored 2-3. **Burning rubber in the car park** signalled Ballesteros's disqualification and departure as he forfeited 13th place money of £1,300.

South African Dale Hayes's challenge for the 1974 Open Championship at Royal Lytham & St. Annes had suffered a slight set-back. A hooked second shot at one hole had sent his ball deep into the clinging rough among the sand dunes. On arrival at the spot, Hayes told his caddie to inform him when they had spent four minutes looking for the ball. The four minutes elapsed without success so Hayes then told his caddie to continue looking for another minute while he moved back down the fairway to the place from where the original errant stroke was struck. On arrival, Hayes dropped another ball but, before he could hit it, there was an **exultant shout from up the fairway** that his first ball had been found. Hayes then picked up the dropped ball and went on to play his original ball.

The incident was seen on television and when Hayes had completed his round and signed his card, the officials were waiting for him. The trouble was that as soon as Hayes had dropped a ball, that ball became the ball in play and the original ball had to be abandoned. Since he had not abandoned the ball, he had played the wrong ball from the wrong place, and as he had not rectified this mistake before making a stroke on the next hole, and since he had also signed his card for a wrong score, there was no alternative but disqualification.

The most famous incident of a **ball being incorrectly replaced on the putting green** occurred in the 1957 Open Championship at St Andrews. Walking towards the final green, Bobby Locke seemed the likely winner, and when he putted up to within two feet of the hole, a three-stroke victory was almost in his grasp. Almost, but not quite, because before Locke putted out, he had to mark his ball to allow his playing companion to finish his round. Locke marked his ball by measuring off one putter's head length to the side. When it was his turn to putt, he duly replaced the ball on the marker and holed out for the fourth Open title of his career. What Locke had failed to do, of course, was replace his marker back in its original spot before replacing his ball. The incident was referred to the Championship Committee which decided that as Locke had gained no advantage by his error, there was no cause for any retrospective action and his winning score should stand.

'Can I have my ball back?' Gordon Brand Jnr awaits a ruling at Moor Park in the 1983 Bob Hope British Classic.

On the 2nd hole at the Muthaiga Club during the final round of the 1980 Kenya Open, Sandy Lyle decided that the **sun's reflection from his putter-head** was more than he could bear. He went to his golf bag, took out a sticking plaster, taped it on the top of the putter and continued with his round. By this action, Lyle was unwittingly in breach of Rule 4-2 which states that, during a stipulated round, the playing characteristics of a club shall not be purposely changed. The infringement was reported to officials by Lyle's playing companion, Nick Faldo, and Lyle was subsequently disqualified. As a result of this incident, the application of coverings on clubs to prevent sun-glare was made allowable since they did not ostensibly change the playing characteristics of a club.

At the 1978 British Amateur Championship at Royal Troon, a match between a Frenchman and a Scotsman was all square coming down the 18th hole. Here the Scotsman hit the green in two shots but the Frenchman cut his approach wildly into some gorse bushes. On reaching his ball, which was virtually unplayable, the Frenchman perceived that a structure specifically erected for the event was standing directly between his ball and the green, so he sent for a ruling. Enter the Englishman, acting in an official capacity. He ruled that since the **structure was in the line of the intended stroke,** the Frenchman was entitled to a free drop out of the bushes.

'Merci beaucoup,' he said, and proceeded to pitch onto the green and hole a long putt for his four.

The Scotsman, upset by this ruling, then three-putted to lose the hole and the match. It later transpired that the ruling given was incorrect since line-of-sight relief is not a Rule of Golf and is only a local rule which is usually applied at professional tournaments where such paraphernalia is to be expected. There was nothing the embarrassed Englishman could do to rectify his mistake, and the match result had to stand.

The introduction of the line-of-sight relief rule at professional tournaments came about as a direct result of an incident in the final of the 1966

Showdown at Wentworth. Jack Nicklaus and Tony Duncan, the referee, in dispute at the 9th.

World Match-Play Championship final between Jack Nicklaus and Gary Player. On the 9th hole at Wentworth, Nicklaus's ball was in deep rough but he felt he was entitled to a free drop because an advertising sign ahead of him was in the line of his recovery. The referee, Colonel Tony Duncan, declined to agree to Nicklaus's request. Nicklaus glowered, Duncan glowered back, neither of them prepared to give an inch. Eventually Nicklaus conceded the hole to Player and angrily marched to the next tee.

'Would you like another referee?' asked Duncan.

'Yes!' retorted Nicklaus, and he and Duncan went their separate ways, each insisting the other was wrong. It was a disastrous day for Nicklaus, who lost the match 6 and 4.

In the 1965 US Amateur Championship, then a 72-hole stroke-play competition, Bob Dickson lost by one stroke to Bob Murphy. Dickson, however, had incurred a four-stroke penalty in the second round for **carrying a fifteenth club** for the first two holes, even though the club did not belong to him and he did not use it. In earlier days, the carrying of extra clubs meant a two-stroke penalty for every hole played in stroke-play and the loss of every hole in match-play. While this penalty was in existence, a situation occurred in the Halford Hewitt foursomes tournament when, in a match, one pair stood five up with seven holes to play only to discover that one of them was carrying more than fourteen clubs. This meant that instead of being five up, they had lost by 10 and 8. The Rule now stands at a maximum four-stroke penalty per round in stroke-play and a maximum two-hole loss per round in match-play.

In the 1937 Ryder Cup at Southport and Ainsdale, Dai Rees played Byron Nelson in the singles. Rees was one up when the pair came to the 11th hole, a par four which they both reached in two shots. Nelson was to putt first and, as was his style, placed the putter-head in front of the ball. There was a sudden gust of wind which **blew the ball into the back of Nelson's putter.** He putted and missed and then Rees missed his birdie try for what appeared to be a half. The referee, however, penalized Nelson a stroke for the ball moving while he was addressing it, and awarded the hole to Rees. This put Rees two up and he won the match by 3 and 1.

INTERNATIONAL INCIDENTS

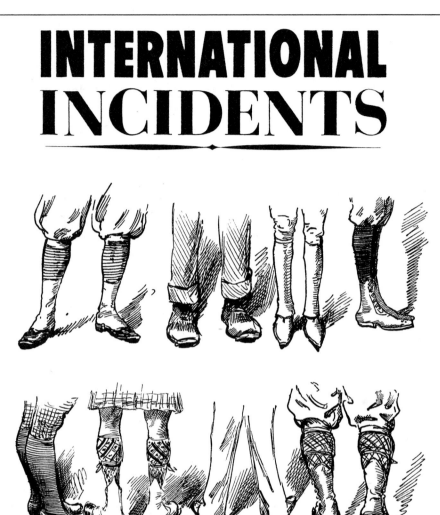

In terms of international golf matches, the only ones with any real relevance are those between Britain and America. The Ryder Cup, the Walker Cup and the Curtis Cup are the contests with the longest pedigree and tradition and it is these encounters which whip the British into a frenzy of national pride.

The Ryder Cup, that elegant little gold chalice presented in 1927 by St Albans seed merchant Sam Ryder, has become the Holy Grail of British professional golf. Since 1979, the contest has been expanded to include players from the Continent of Europe so the match is really between the two major professional Tours in the world. In the 25 stagings of the Ryder Cup until 1983, the British have won three times to the Americans' 21 victories with one tie. Many results have been desperately close but it has invariably been the British who have wilted. The same story applies in the Walker Cup and Curtis Cup, for men and women amateurs respectively.

Any selection of the **most tragic British moment** must be subjective but one whose pain has not been erased by the passing years concerns the 1953 Ryder Cup at Wentworth. As usual, another American victory looked safe as they led the foursomes 3 – 1. A spirited fight-back by the British in the singles saw the match tied with the outcome resting on the two singles involving Peter Alliss and Bernard Hunt, the two youngest members of the side. What happened next marked both of them for the remainder of their playing days. First Alliss came to the final hole one down against Jim Turnesa, having missed a short putt to lose the 16th and driven out-of-bounds to lose the 17th. On the 18th, Turnesa drove into the trees, hacked out and was still short of the green in three. Meanwhile, Alliss was just left of the green, pin-high, in two. Inexperienced and unaccustomed to the pressures, he fluffed his little chip, chipped again to around a

Our brave lads set forth from Waterloo Station for the States to compete in the first Ryder Cup match in 1927. Left to right: George Duncan, Archie Compston, Ted Ray, F. Robson, Sam Ryder (without hat but with dog), George Gadd, C.A. Whitcombe, Arthur Havers, A. Mitchell and G. Philpott (manager).

yard, and with Turnesa making a six, needed that putt to halve the match. He missed it. Shortly afterwards, Hunt arrived on the same green needing two putts to win his match against Dave Douglas but three-putted to halve. Great Britain and Ireland lost the match $6\frac{1}{2}$ – $5\frac{1}{2}$.

More final-green agony befell Britain in the 1984 Curtis Cup match at Muirfield. The British had hounded the Americans all the way and, with only one singles to be decided, a halved match would mean the Cup would be shared. Ultimately, Penny Grice, a sturdy Yorkshire lass, faced a putt of four feet on the last green to win the hole, halve her match and ensure the tie. The ball hit the hole and stayed out.

A distraught Penny Grice at Muirfield in the 1984 Curtis Cup.

The oldest of the three trophies, the Walker Cup, began in 1922 but has provided the British with scant success. Until 1983, the Americans have won 26 times to two British victories with one epic tie. No British team in any of the trophy matches has ever won on American soil but in 1965, at Five Farms near Baltimore, history was nearly made. The British led by five matches with eight singles left to play. On a grisly afternoon for the British, the home side won six of the singles and lost one, and the outcome depended on the match between John Hopkins of the USA and Britain's Clive Clark. Hopkins was one up on the 17th tee, a short hole, and proceeded to shank his tee shot into the trees. He found the green with his second and then holed cruelly for the half. On the final green, Clark faced a downhill putt of 35 feet to win the hole and tie the Walker Cup. Incredibly he holed it, causing his team captain, Irishman Joe Carr, to rush over saying:

'You moved your head, you moved your body, how the hell did you move the hole to catch your ball?'

Clark's effort remains the **longest putt holed to save defeat.**

The British teams in the 1928 and 1961 Walker Cups and the 1947 Ryder Cup all lost by 11 matches to 1 – **the heaviest defeats to date.** Whitewashes were prevented by singles victories by Tony Torrance and Martin Christmas in the Walker Cup and Sam King in the Ryder Cup. In the 1936 Walker Cup, Britain did not win a single match but gained $1\frac{1}{2}$ points from three halved matches.

As the 1974 American Amateur Champion, Jerry Pate was a member of the 1975 US Walker Cup team at St Andrews. Pate played four times, two foursomes and two singles, and lost on each occasion – **the worst American début.** He completed an unhappy visit by losing in the first round of the British Amateur Championship the week after the Walker Cup.

The most under-utilized internationals were George Gadd (1927), Eric Green (1947), Reg Horne (1947), Laurie Ayton (1949) and Jack Hargreaves (1951). All were selected for the Great Britain and Ireland Ryder Cup team but did not play a match. John Garner (1971–73) was selected twice but only played one match, which he lost.

The most destructive international shot was fired in the 1932 Walker Cup at The Country Club, Brookline, Massachusetts. British player Leonard Crawley overhit his second shot to the 18th and the ball struck and dented the Walker Cup itself as it stood on display.

The spirit of international goodwill, which is supposed to be engendered by the staging of the Ryder, Walker and Curtis Cups, is sometimes stretched. It has to be said that any 'aggro' has usually emanated from the American camp, while the British have been content to be seen as jolly good sports. On the eve of the 1949 Ryder Cup at Ganton, US captain Ben Hogan lodged a complaint about the form and make of the iron clubs belonging to two British players. After five hours of discussion, it was finally agreed that the grooves in the offending clubs be filed down.

A **most acrimonious encounter** took place in the 1957 Ryder Cup at Lindrick, scene of Britain's last victory to date. In the singles, Eric Brown comprehensively dismissed American Tommy Bolt by 4 and 3. Bolt refused to shake hands with Brown, saying he hadn't enjoyed the match at all.

'I don't suppose you did,' retorted Brown, 'because you never had an earthly hope of beating me.'

Brown never lost a singles match in four Ryder Cup appearances, a record by a British player recently matched by Nick Faldo (1977–83).

The dramatic tie in the 1969 Ryder Cup at Royal Birkdale also produced some **sour moments**. In a four-ball match involving Bernard Gallacher and Brian Huggett against Americans Dave Hill and Ken Still, the Americans putted out of turn on one green. The British, who were quite within their rights, asked the Americans to replay the stroke. In a fit of pique, the Americans picked up their ball and conceded the hole to the British.

The climax of this extraordinary contest came when Jack Nicklaus and Tony Jacklin came up the final hole with the match tied and their singles standing at all square. Both hit the green in two shots and Nicklaus putted first, leaving his ball some four feet past the hole. Jacklin putted up to within three feet. Nicklaus then holed his putt and graciously conceded Jacklin his putt. The American captain, Sam Snead, was not impressed by Nicklaus's sporting concession and harsh words were exchanged in the locker-room afterwards.

The business of conceding putts left a **nasty taste** in a PGA Cup match between Britain and America which is a contest between the club professionals of both countries. In one year, during a four-ball match, the British missed a birdie putt to win a hole and the player unconsciously raked the ball back,

Ructions at the 1969 Ryder Cup at Royal Birkdale. Dave Hill and Brian Huggett exchange words while Bernard Gallacher looks on.

thinking he had obtained a half. The Americans however, as they had every right to do, claimed the hole. Stung by this display of 'international goodwill', the British fought back to halve that particular match and went on to tie the entire encounter.

Of all the representative matches between the two countries, there is one Cup which transcends all the others, a match in which many vital fluids are shed, where the honour of playing for one's country is put above mere financial gain and the Olympic ideal is still maintained. Despite the profession of the combatants, or perhaps because of it, this match receives little publicity, but since its inception in 1980 it has created more drama, more excitement and more slapstick comedy than any of the three main Cups put together.

The annual **Writer Cup** between the golfing press of Britain and America is where real golf comes into its own. The matches do not feature sensational bursts of sub-par scoring, no birdie barrages – indeed, individual matches are more likely to be won by careful adjustment of handicaps and a capacity to absorb large amounts of local firewater and still remain perpendicular. Yet, in 1983, the British team achieved what no other preceding side from these shores had ever achieved. As holders of the trophy, they retained the cup on American soil.

Where the match took place must remain a secret since the club involved is still concerned about the effect any publicity might have on its tourist trade, but it was somewhere in South Carolina. After two days of gruelling competition, the Americans led by one point with one singles still on the course. This match involved the highest-handicap members of each side, Jim Stewart of America and Bill Blighton of Britain, playing that day off 36 and 30 respectively. Blighton had fought back from three down to only one down by the 16th when his composure was shattered by the sight of a milling horde of team-mates descending on his match with the dreadful news that the result depended on him.

His situation looked bleak when, on the 16th, a short hole, his opponent was bunkered in one by the green while he had taken five strokes to reach the putting surface. Much later, very much later, the American was still in the bunker and eventually conceded the hole. The 17th was halved and so the stage was set for the *dénouement*.

The final hole required a carry from the tee of some 125 yards across a lake. Egged on by his team-mates, Blighton launched himself at his ball, sending it **skipping across the water like a bouncing bomb** until it came to rest near the far bank, still submerged. Stewart took an alternative route and craftily sent his tee shot into a grove of trees. His next attempt hit a tree and bounced into the undergrowth and was lost. Dropping another ball, he sent it right across the fairway into another patch of rubbish. Meanwhile, Blighton tried to extricate his ball from the water. He failed to make any contact with his first effort but managed to hack the ball half-way up the bank on the next try. His fourth shot sent the ball up the fairway but still more than 300 yards from the green. A series of hacks in the undergrowth from Stewart followed until, finally, he had taken enough. He conceded the hole and the match so the contest was tied. **Britain retained the Cup and history was made.**

GRIEVOUS BODILY GOLF: A BIZARRE RECORD

MOST SELF-DESTRUCTIVE GOLFERS

American professional Lefty Stackhouse used to take it out on himself if he hit a poor shot. If he hooked the ball he would go to a nearby tree and punish his erring hand by smashing it against the trunk. On another occasion he punched himself on the chin, knocking himself out. Once, after a bad round, he calmly signed his card, paid off his caddie, put his clubs in the car and then retired to a nearby rose garden where he thrashed around among the thorns, lacerating himself so badly that he had to receive medical attention.

In Australia, a lady golfer was so excited over the outcome of a shot that she threw up her hands, stepped back and tripped over her golf bag, breaking both her arms. In Texas, golfer Moody Weaver took a practice swing with such force that he broke his leg in two places.

UNLUCKIEST INJURIES

Most self-inflicted wounds which occur on the golf course are purely mental. There is little physical danger, apart from being struck by someone else's errant golf ball, so it would seem that a walk round a golf course should be relatively injury-free. This assumption does not, however, take into account the enormous capacity golfers have for providing the exceptions to every rule. To continue:

On Friday 13 February 1981, Helen Bopp broke an arm while taking a swing on the Villa de Paz course in Arizona. The accident occurred on the 13th hole.

Bob Russell of Ohio took a practice swing one day in 1974 and sent up a cloud of smoke; at the same time he felt a searing pain in his leg. It transpired that the clubhead had detonated a .22 cartridge hidden in the grass.

MOST COURTEOUS ASSAILANT

On the 72nd hole of the 1971 Open at Royal Birkdale, Liang-Huan Lu, known as 'Mr Lu', hooked his second shot into the crowd, the ball striking a lady spectator who, as a result, had to be taken to hospital. Although shaken by the incident, Mr Lu pitched onto the green and holed the putt to finish second behind Lee Trevino. Later Mr Lu visited his victim in hospital and, presenting her with a box of golf balls, said in broken English: 'Now you throw at me.'

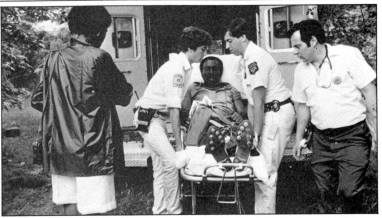

Overcome by heat, Calvin Peete is stretchered off during the 1984 US Open Championship.

MOST DANGEROUS GREEN

The island green of the 132-yard 17th at the Tournament Players' Club in Florida has, in its short history, become a notorious watery graveyard for golf balls. The hole is also quite dangerous if your ball actually lands on the green, for in its first year of play no less than three people finished in the water as they stepped back to survey the line of a putt.

BIGGEST TUMBLE

In the quarter-finals of the 1979 English Amateur Championship at Royal St George's, Reg Glading was forced into extra holes. On the 22nd, or fourth extra hole, Glading saw his drive pitch into the cavernous bunker which guards the right-hand side of the fairway. When he arrived at the bunker, his ball was plugged right at the top of this immense dune. In the manner of a Sherpa, Glading clambered up to his ball with a club. He made fast his stance, took a swing, overblanced and fell back some twenty-five feet to the bottom of the bunker, somersaulting twice. The ball followed him down, struck him, and he had to concede the hole and the match.

MOST FATAL STROKES

Edward Harrison was playing alone at the Inglewood Country Club in Seattle when the shaft of his driver broke and pierced his groin. He collapsed and bled to death about 100 yards from the 9th tee where the accident occurred. Rudolph Roy was killed at a Montreal course when, as he attempted to play out of some trees, the shaft of his club broke, rebounded off a tree and the jagged edge plunged into his body.

MOST WAYWARD GOLFING POLITICIAN

In the 1970 Bob Hope Classic in Palm Springs, the then Vice-President Spiro Agnew drove from the 1st tee, caught the ball on the toe of the club and hit his professional partner, Doug Sanders, causing a one-inch gash. The round continued with Agnew inflicting further carnage, this time on the crowd. A hooked shot over the gallery was followed by a slice into the gallery, the ball winging one man and downing his wife as well. The following year, Agnew struck a woman spectator who had to be admitted to hospital suffering from severe bruising.

MOST SHORT-LIVED MOMENT OF JOY

Playing in the 1934 US Open at Merion, Bobby Cruickshank topped his second shot to the 11th green. The ball was heading for a water hazard but struck a rock and bounced onto the green. In his jubilation, Cruickshank threw his club into the air but forgot that what goes up, must come down. It did, right on top of his head, knocking him senseless to the ground.

NUTTIEST DRIVER

Greg Sonnenfeld hit a poor tee shot during the 1984 Natal Amateur Championship, and in disgust threw his driver into a tree where it lodged among the branches. A thoroughly embarrassed Sonnenfeld then clambered up into the branches to retrieve the club whereupon it fell on his head, and he had to go to the local hospital for stitches to be inserted.

WORST SCORE WHILE INJURED

When American professional Mike Reasor made the cut in the 1974 Tallahassee Open he knew he was exempt from pre-qualifying for the next tournament, provided he completed the final two rounds. Due to an arm injury incurred after the first 36 holes, Reasor had to play the remaining 36 using just one arm. He scored 123 and 114 but he was in the next tournament.

BOUNCIEST BALL

In the 1952 Los Angeles Open, competitor Bud Hoelscher hit a wild second shot to the 18th green. The ball struck a cameraman on the head, inflicting a scalp wound, bounced onto a can of water, up into the face of an official and landed on the green.

A young scoreboard carrier receives attention after being struck by a drive from Philip Parkin at the British Youths' Golf Championship at Sunningdale in 1983.

BRAVEST RECOVERY

American professional Greg Powers was playing in the Greater Eyrie Pennsylvania Charity Classic when his tee shot on the 8th hole came to rest behind a tree, leaving him very little room to follow-through. He tried to hit a crisp 3-iron but the club hit the tree, the shaft snapped and the club-head whipped round and smacked him on the forehead. He was unconscious for about five minutes and was advised by a doctor to discontinue his round. He refused and carried on, holding an ice-pack to his injured head between shots, and finished with a score of 65.

BIGGEST DRIP

Junior golf competition organizers do not welcome doting parents as caddies for their offspring. In the 1951 Boys' Championship at Prestwick this feeling was not so prevalent but one father probably wished it was. While endeavouring to retrieve one of his son's misdirected strokes, Dad fell head first into the Pow Burn which was in full spate after heavy rain. He extricated himself and abandoned his paternal duties, returning instead to his hotel to dry out.

MOST PUNCTURED GOLFER

Joe Franzese's false teeth felt uncomfortable during a round at the Kanajoharie Country Club in New York State, so he took the teeth out, wrapped them in a handkerchief and put them in his back pocket. A few holes later his playing companion hit a shot off-line and the ball struck Joe right on his teeth-filled back pocket. He wasn't hurt but his teeth were broken. Further investigations behind some bushes revealed that he had suffered other injuries to a more tender part of his anatomy – he had been bitten on the backside by his own teeth.

WETTEST DRIVE

Playing the 6th hole at Lewes GC, Sussex, A. W. Good approached his second shot with his ball lying close to a sheep trough which served the animals on the course. He put rather too much effort into his swing and overbalanced into the trough which was full of water.

THE SIMPLE ACT OF PUTTING

No other aspect of the game has received more attention than putting. This small act on a simple scale is the crunch area of golf, the stroke that finally makes the difference between victory and defeat. The knowledge that there is no chance of recovery from a missed putt has driven strong men to drink, nervous breakdowns and the divorce courts. It has also produced a depressing chronicle of tragedy, moments of black farce and spells of numbing ineptitude – the latter being more commonly referred to as the 'yips', 'jerks' or 'twitch'.

Many famous players have been afflicted by the 'yips', including Ben Hogan, Sam Snead, Arnold Palmer and Tony Jacklin and, in each of their cases, the disease came about after many years of tournament grind during which time the fear of failure had overcome the desire for victory. It was therefore generally accepted that **victims of the involuntary spasm** were veteran performers whose nerves had been shredded. That theory was destroyed in 1976 by the appearance of West Germany's Bernhard Langer.

In the Hennessy Cognac Cup match of that year, Langer made his début for the Continent against the British. Through the green, Langer's game was a match for anyone, but on the green he was pitiful. Spectators turned away in embarrassment as Langer displayed one of the most serious cases of the 'yips' ever witnessed. Putts of three feet would often finish six feet past the hole as the involuntary spasm accelerated the putter-head at uncontrollable speed towards the ball. At the age of nineteen, Langer had demonstrated that the 'yips' can strike at any age. The acquisition of a new putter in 1980 helped stem the tide for Langer and he has subsequently developed into a formidable competitor who holes his fair share of putts. Occasionally, as in cases of malaria, the parasite in his system emerges for a frolic with his psyche as it did in the 1982 PGA Championship at Hillside when, in the final round, Langer four-putted the 16th green, an extravagance which put him in a play-off with Tony Jacklin which the latter won.

Of course, four-putts are common in the professional game but a particularly curious instance occurred in the 1955 US Masters at Augusta National. Davis Love, now a respected teacher, came to the 9th hole at level par for the tournament. His approach shot to this cantilevered green finished sixty feet above the hole. His first putt ran down the slope, past the hole, off the green and fifteen feet back down the fairway. He chipped back and then took three more putts. This could be regarded as a

Joshua Crane employing his eighteen-inch putter during the Open Championship at Sandwich in 1928. The sceptical wagging of innumerable heads seemed subsequently justified by Crane's headlong rush out of the competition.

The bitter taste of a missed putt. Tony Jacklin at the 1982 Sun Alliance PGA Championship which he eventually won.

four-putt green plus one.

       Not so common in professional golf is the seven-putt green – but it's been done. During the World Series tournament at Firestone, Jerry Pate reached the front edge of the green at the 2nd hole in two shots. His first putt finished four feet past the hole, the second attempt three feet past while his third was close but lipped out. He back-handed the ball to knock it into the hole but hit it too hard – the ball jumped over the hole and struck him on the foot. The two-stroke penalty he incurred meant he finally **holed out in nine.**

       Even rarer in professional golf, or any other standard for that matter, is the 12-putt green but again, sorry to report, it's been done. In the 1968 French Open at St Cloud, Brian Barnes missed a short putt and, in anger and frustration, attempted to rake the ball back into the hole. The ball once again eluded its target and Barnes's spleen gave vent to a fresh upsurge of bile. In a fury, he danced around the hole, patting the ball to and fro, at one stage in his mad quadrille standing astride the line of his putt to incur a further two-stroke penalty. The ball finally disappeared on the twelfth stroke to give Barnes a score of 15 for the hole and no further interest in the outcome of the tournament.

       However, these attempts fall well short of the World Record for **most putts taken on one green.** The record-holder is A. J. Lewis who, while playing in a competition at Peacehaven, Sussex in 1890, took 156 putts on a green without holing out.

'Come on Lord!'   *'Please!'*   *'Hallelujah!'*
Jeff Hawkes invokes the ultimate outside agency for an eagle 3 in the 1982 Coral Classic.

Against Mr Lewis's awe-inspiring display can be placed the feat of Gordie Franza of Rochester, New York during a putting contest held at Pinehurst, North Carolina in 1981. He set the record for **most consecutive putts holed** when he holed 354 successive putts of four feet. Franza, a 9-handicapper, putted for more than two hours before the 355th putt lipped out.

But it is in the white-heat of major competition that putting agonies manifest themselves in their most hideous form. Doug Sanders's tragic miss from two feet on the final green of the 1970 Open Championship at St Andrews is generally regarded as the most heart-breaking, but shorter, much shorter, putts have failed to find the target. In the 1889 Open at Musselburgh, Andrew Kirkaldy, playing the 14th hole in the final round, went to knock in a one-inch putt and missed the ball completely. He eventually tied with Willie Park for the title but lost the play-off. Harry Vardon produced a similar air-shot in the 1900 US Open when he missed the ball on a six-inch putt – although he still won.

More recently was the third round aberration by Hale Irwin in the 1983 Open at Royal Birkdale. On the 14th green of that round, Irwin went to back-hand the ball on the edge of the hole and failed to make contact. Inevitably, he finished one stroke behind the winner, Tom Watson.

That was the **Year of the**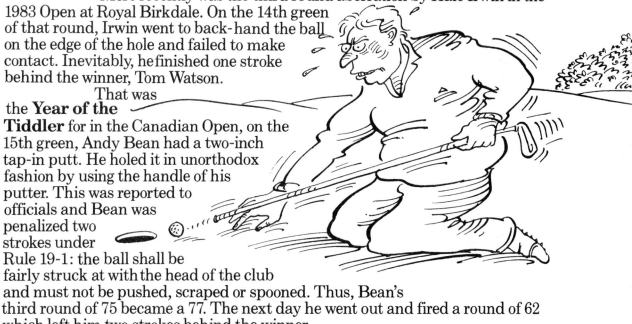
Tiddler for in the Canadian Open, on the 15th green, Andy Bean had a two-inch tap-in putt. He holed it in unorthodox fashion by using the handle of his putter. This was reported to officials and Bean was penalized two strokes under Rule 19-1: the ball shall be fairly struck at with the head of the club and must not be pushed, scraped or spooned. Thus, Bean's third round of 75 became a 77. The next day he went out and fired a round of 62 which left him two strokes behind the winner.

Tommy Horton was another victim of some putting tomfoolery which occurred in the 1984 Kenya Open. As the final round progressed, Horton became more and more frustrated by his inability to hole putts. Like many golfers, he vented his anger on the putter, in this case by banging it sharply against a rock. The putter did not take kindly to this treatment and the head was loosened from the shaft, so for the remaining few holes Horton **putted with the head clanking about** as it struck the ball. On the final green, he missed yet another putt and then removed the shaft from the head and holed out using just the head. This act, which was intended as a bit of fun, was not so amusing afterwards. Having already signed his card, Horton found himself disqualified under Rule 4-1 which states that the club shall be composed of a shaft and head and all parts should be fixed so that the club is one unit.

Lanny Wadkins demonstrates his Indian putter trick.

In the 1977 Open Championship at Turnberry, American professional Mark Hayes, using a cross-handed grip on his putter, broke the record for the Championship with a 63 which contained numerous lengthy holed putts. The gods of golf do not take kindly to such excesses and noted Hayes down in their log-book as one to take care of later. It took them two years to strike back. In the 1979 Crosby tournament at Pebble Beach, Hayes led the field by three strokes with four holes to play. On the 15th green he four-putted from seven feet and then three-putted the 16th. He tied for the title with Andy Bean and Lon Hinkle and lost the play-off to Hinkle. Further indignity was heaped upon Hayes in the 1982 US Masters. On the 18th hole, his approach shot finished six feet above the hole and his first putt just shaved the cup. The hole was cut on the top of a sharp slope and Hayes's ball failed to stop. It gathered pace down the hill, finally coming to rest at the foot. His next putt was from 40 feet. He made a good try at it, the ball running up past the hole and then curving away to run back down the hill again to arrive at his feet. By now some unseemly sniggering was emanating from the gallery and the acutely embarrassed Hayes had another stab. This time he managed to stop the ball just short of the hole and, **rushing up the slope to hit it again** before it slid back, holed out in six.

Max Faulkner and his famous putter made from a piece of driftwood and a billiard cue.

In the 1927 Halford-Hewitt, the annual public school old boys foursomes competition held at Deal, a match between Winchester and Harrow arrived at the 19th green with Winchester having three putts from twelve feet for victory. Wykehamist Major Thorburn addressed the first putt by placing his putter in front of the ball as a preliminary to his stroke. At this moment he was smitten by an involuntary spasm and jerked the putter backwards, sending the ball several yards further away from the hole. Three more putts followed and Winchester could only halve the hole; they lost at the 20th.

In this age of semi-literate utterances by the world's leading players, e.g. 'I drove it real good but putted it bad' or 'I golfed my ball real good out there and made a bunch of putts', let us ponder on these words of Hubert Green who, with this **stunning piece of logic**, brought a new dimension to the old, hackneyed putting cliché of 'Never up, never in'.

'Ninety-five per cent of putts which finish short,' said Hubert, 'don't go in.'

FAMOUS HORROR HOLES

Over the years, certain holes on famous courses have achieved notoriety for the consistent retribution they exact. These golfing blackspots have been, and will doubtless continue to be, the most likely places where players experience a monumental crash. The universal ingredient in all of them is temptation – they challenge the golfer to bite off just that little piece more than can be safely chewed, and the consequences of doing that are invariably sickening.

In terms of **highest dyspepsia rating** and most bilious attacks suffered by the world's great players, the 17th or Road Hole at St Andrews deserves an article in *The Lancet*. There is a disaster story for every one of its 461 yards, but in order to keep this litany of woe in manageable proportions it is necessary to concentrate on the more epic catastrophes. Travelling back in time, we alight at St Andrews just at the closing stages of the 1885 Open Championship. The course is buzzing with excitement as local man David Ayton steps on to the 17th tee with a comfortable lead. Two good shots towards the green leave Ayton with a straightforward chip and run to the hole. The chip is slightly underhit and fails to hold the crested green and runs back to finish in front of the Road Bunker, a pot hole of perdition if ever there was one. Ayton's next shot clears the bunker and also clears the green to finish on the road. The next one rolls up the bank, stops tantalizingly at the top and rolls back down. This time Ayton makes sure he gets over the bank but overhits into the bunker. Three attempts later he finally gets onto the green, two-putts for an eleven and loses the Championship by two strokes.

An unnerving spectator.

The road to ruin. Sam King negotiates the 17th at St Andrews during the 1955 Open Championship.

Closer to us in time was the play-off for the 1935 R & A Autumn Medal. Raymond Oppenheimer, the distinguished amateur international, was only a stroke behind his opponent on the 17th tee. **Several tee shots later** that deficit had been hugely increased as Oppenheimer holed out in eleven.

More recent memories are provided by the 1978 Open Championship when the Road Hole numbered among its victims Arnold Palmer, who drove out-of-bounds on two successive days to take seven each time, and Severiano Ballesteros who drove out-of-bounds at the end of his second round to take six.

The man who grabbed all the limelight, however, was Japanese professional Tsuneyuki Nakajima. In the spring of the same year, Nakajima had carved his unpronounceable name on the long list of disasters pertaining to another famous horror hole – the 13th at Augusta National. In the US Masters that April he had taken thirteen for the hole but, to be fair, that score contained five penalty strokes so he had only actually hit the ball eight times. Golf is a great leveller and Nakajima had every right to feel that the game owed him something. It did. On the 17th hole of his third round in the 1978 Open Championship, Nakajima **hit his ball nine times without any penalty strokes.** It happened like this. Two good shots found his ball on the left-hand edge of the green, leaving him a long putt up and across the crest towards the pin. His expression after his first putt was one of total disbelief. The ball rolled up the crest and then, losing momentum, trickled back down into the Road Bunker. It took him four more bunker shots to regain the putting surface and two more putts to get the ball into the hole. In the 1984 Open Championship at St Andrews he was asked what he thought of the 17th. He replied:

BANZAI!

'Very tough – like Mrs Thatcher.'

From calamity towards the end of a round, let us move back down the course to a couple of starting holes where a calculator is sometimes required. There is no tougher opening hole than the 1st at Hoylake. The chief feature of the hole is the famous 'cop' or turfed wall which surrounds the practice ground and denotes an out-of-bounds area within the confines of the course. The hole is a right-angled dog-leg with the cop threatening both the drive and the second shot. In the 1930 Open Championship there, competitor A. Tingey got his drive safely away and then proceded to hit three successive approach shots over the cop. It was an unfair cop for Tingey, who holed out in eleven.

The hole was also the scene of a particularly dramatic interlude when it was played as the 19th by Horace Hutchinson and Bernard Darwin in the 1910 Amateur Championship. Both players drove safely and then both put two shots out-of-bounds. Drawing on some hidden reserve, Hutchinson kept his next shot in play but Darwin's swing was repeating with unerring consistency and his third attempt met the same fate as his previous two. He conceded the hole and the match.

The 1st at Prestwick is another opening hole with its fair share of melodrama. The railway from Ayr to Glasgow runs parallel along its entire length and the stories are legion of competitors going out of bounds more than once as they played it. In the 1934 Amateur Championship, two players both drove onto the railway. Both reloaded onto the fairway and then both sent their second shots back out-of-bounds. In his writings, the same Bernard Darwin (see above) recalls how one player going out in a medal hit his tee shot onto the railway whence it bounced back into play. He repeated the stroke on his second shot only this time the ball **not only bounced back off the railway but finished in the hole.** 'After this rather fortunate two,' wrote Darwin, 'he pulled himself together and won the competition.'

You might think that short holes would have no place in this Chamber of Horrors but, of course, you'd be wrong and, if you want confirmation, have a word with German amateur Hermann Tissies. As a young man, Hermann was playing in the 1950 Open Championship at Troon and succeeded in placing his name in the record books for the second highest score in the history of the Championship. Moreover it was achieved on the shortest hole in championship golf, the 126-yard 8th or 'Postage Stamp'. Hermann failed to lick it because, first, his tee shot landed in one of the three pot bunkers which guard the green. He then committed, as *The Scotsman* reported at the time, **'a horrible species of ping-pong played between the bunkers'.** One bunker cost him five strokes before his ball sought sanctuary in another. He eventually extricated his ball onto the green after twelve strokes and, very creditably in the circumstances, only took three putts for a massive fifteen.

If you still want confirmation of short-hole horrors, then have a chat with Tom Weiskopf about the 12th at Augusta National – but only if you're practised at wrestling grizzly bears or enjoy sitting atop Mt Etna just before she is about to erupt. The 12th at Augusta is 155 yards long, played to a narrow green fronted by a broad creek. The hole requires careful club selection since a capricious wind can play tricks with the ball in flight. In the first round of the 1980 US Masters, Weiskopf fell victim to indecision and dumped his tee shot in the creek. He walked forward to the ball-dropping zone and dropped another ball. He pitched the ball into the water. He reached out to his caddie for another ball and dropped it. He pitched it into the water. Like an automaton, Weiskopf continued to reach for another ball, drop it and pitch into the water. In all, **he put five balls into the creek** and eventually walked off the green with a thirteen marked on his card. The next day Weiskopf cracked it – he scored seven on the 12th.

The most photographed short hole in the world is undoubtedly the 16th at Cypress Point. If it were located in a field just outside Waco, Texas then no photographer would bother removing his lens cap, but put its 233 yards on the Monterey Peninsula in California, and its green on a rocky promontory and separate the green from the tee with the Pacific Ocean and you have a hole which demands rolls of film. It also demands a tee shot combining power and precision if the carry is to be made. There is an alternative route to a patch of fairway to the left and short of the green but no golfer worth his salt could resist the temptation to see the ball soaring out across the blue waters and plummetting down onto the green.

When temptation beckons, disaster is not far behind, and since the US Tour stopped regularly at Cypress Point for the Bing Crosby tournaments, the casualty list is formidable. The record for the highest score on the hole is nineteen, set by Hans Merrell in the 1959 Crosby. Merrell's tee shot failed to make the carry and his ball landed at the foot of the cliffs among the ice-plant which flourishes in the prevailing moist conditions. Now, the ice-plant is of the genus Mesembryanthemum but otherwise bears little relationship to the flowers you might plant in your garden. The ice-plant's leaves possess the consistency of tungsten and require a chain-saw to cut through them. Merrell did not have a chain-saw, he had a golf club and its cutting edge had been severely blunted by the time he finally got his ball up onto the green. Henry Ransom, a strong and violent man (see 'The Violent Game') was another who failed to crop the ice-plant but he, the quitter, packed up after sixteen attempts. The late Guy Wolstenholme slipped and fell, **breaking his arm when clambering down the cliffs,** drawing the comment from Arnold Palmer:

'I knew it was a tough hole but I didn't think it could break your arm.'

Unlike Ransom, Ed 'Porky' Oliver didn't know when to quit when he hit three tee-shots to the base of the cliffs before landing his fourth drive on grass. Undaunted, Oliver climbed down to play his first drive. Forty minutes later he staggered back, soaked and scratched, to be met by the tournament host, Bing Crosby.

'How many to clear the cliffs?' asked Crosby. 'Five hits?'

Oliver shook his head.

'Ten?'

Steam began to emanate from Oliver's ears.

'Don't tell me you took an even dozen?' inquired Crosby, unaware of the torment.

'It took me 16 strokes to hole out,' screamed Oliver, 'and get away from me you damned crooner!' Oliver's card for the round recorded a bottom-heavy 38 out, 50 in.

The Chakrata links in the Himalayas, 1899.

ANIMAL CRACKERS

Due to its proximity to nature, it is inevitable that golf will produce its fair share of clashes with the various flora and fauna which abound on the course. The tendency golfers have to hit a golf ball into dense undergrowth means that the battle is unceasing, with nature usually gaining the upper hand. Crows, snakes, squirrels, gophers, foxes, badgers and geese have all demonstrated a liking for golf balls, probably in the mistaken belief that they are eggs. One gopher in Canada set an unofficial world record for hoarding when its nest was discovered to contain 250 balls. Crows have been observed dropping balls from great heights in an attempt to smash them.

A notorious crow frequented the 13th hole at the Wilmslow course in Cheshire, regularly carrying off balls. One of its victims was professional Doug McClelland who was robbed during the Greater Manchester Open, while in the same area, at Hoylake, a group of crows relieved the members of 26 brand new balls in a single day. On another occasion, a player drove his ball down the fairway but as he walked towards his shot he could not see the ball anywhere. He approached a hen sitting in the middle of the fairway whereupon the hen, another egg-deluded creature, got up to reveal the player's ball.

In the struggle for air supremacy, golfers have registered 'kills' on crows, seagulls, hawks, pigeons and ducks. The prize in the category of **most appropriate shot** must surely go to Willie Fraser of Kingussie GC, then aged 11, who, on 12 August 1975 (The Glorious Twelfth) killed a grouse with his tee shot.

Meanwhile, back on the ground the most spectacular kill was recorded in 1934 at St Margarets-at-Cliffe GC, Kent when the professional, W. J. Robinson, killed a cow with his tee shot at the 18th. The animal was struck on the back of the head, fell, got up, staggered 50 yards and then dropped stone dead. One can only surmise that the shot was powerfully struck albeit a little low.

Bovine revenge was extracted 47 years later in Oakland, California when a bull escaped from a stockyard and ran onto the nearby Gailbraith GC and chased golfer Robert Warren. Warren ran for a tree but the bull anticipated this move and arrived at the tree simultaneously with Warren. A hefty butt from the bull ensued and Warren was stretchered off with a broken leg.

If you think that's a load of bull, then this incident may stretch your credibility even further. On the 145-yard 4th hole at the Mountain View GC in Oregon, Ted Bowenhouse shanked his 7-iron tee shot over a barbed wire fence into a field. The ball ricocheted off the forehead of a grazing

GOOD SHOT! HE'S OVER THE BUNKER

cow, bounced back onto the course, hit a sprinkler head then struck a mower parked by the side of the green. From there its only possible destination was the bottom of the cup where, indeed, it finished.

A resident mole at the 198-yard 5th hole at Brampton GC, Cumbria made an ill-timed and subsequently fatal appearance for as it poked its snout above ground it was despatched to that Great Molehill in the Sky by a ball struck with a 3-wood. The golfer, Bill Writson, was credited with **golf's only known mole-in-one.**

The old joke about the golfer thrashing about in the rough and then claiming he was killing a snake has a ring of truth in it so far as Jimmy Stewart is concerned. Playing in the 1972 Singapore Open, Stewart approached his ball on one hole only to see a large cobra converging on the missile. He killed the reptile with a club only to see another, smaller cobra emerge from the dead snake's jaws. It met the same fate.

On certain up-country courses in Africa, caddies refuse to venture into the long rough for fear of snakebite, while in the United States the city council of Arkansas City, Kansas ask golfers playing the Springhill course to sign a release freeing the city from liability in case of snakebite. At the Glen Canyon course in Arizona a local rule provides that 'If your ball lands within a club length of a rattlesnake you are allowed to move the ball.'

Nature had the last word at a water-strewn hole in Portugal. The water came into play on two adjacent

It's a dog's life for Kruger, an Essex Doberman pinscher, whose appetite for golf balls resulted in seven having to be removed from his stomach.

holes and was also the home of a group of ducks. One day the ducks were going peacefully about their business when two four-balls arrived at the holes together. Shot after shot plunged into the water around the ducks until finally they could take the barrage no longer and, almost as one, waddled out of the water, taking refuge in the safer confines of the green the golfers were aiming at.

A place in Irish folklore is reserved for **the goats of Lahinch.** Successive generations of these animals have acted as reliable weather forecasters for golfers on this County Clare links. When the weather is set fair, the goats can be found on the far reaches of the course but if the weather is about to change for the worse, the goats will head back to shelter in the lee of the clubhouse. On one occasion the club barometer broke down, whereupon the Secretary pinned up a notice which read: 'See Goats'. In recent years the goats have been elevated to a position on the official club crest. No such honour was given to a ram which attacked two players approaching the 7th green at Dungannon Links, Co Tyrone in 1936. Despite their attempts to beat off the aggressive ruminant, they were forced to give up their game.

Apart from dogs, which are *de trop* at tournaments, professional golfers are fairly well protected from interference by animal outside agencies, but not always. In the 1968 Open Championship at Carnoustie, British professional John Morgan had the unnerving experience of being bitten by a rat while looking for a ball in the rough. He was also bitten by the golf course – he was round in 92.

It was P. G. Wodehouse who wrote of the golfer whose game was affected by 'the clamour of the butterflies in the adjoining meadow' but one golfer who has cause to curse this particular species of wildlife is British professional Ian Mosey. In the 1979 South African

Angel Gallardo and "loose impediment" at the World Cup Championship, Palm Beach in 1971.

Open he stood on the final tee needing a par four to win the title. As he began his downswing on the drive, **a butterfly alighted on his ball** causing him to hit it into the trees. He eventually holed out in six, missing a putt of a yard to tie.

One professional who succeeded in levelling up the scores a little in man's struggle against nature was Nick Price. Playing at the Elephant Hills course on the banks of the Zambesi in Zimbabwe, Price drove off at one hole just as a group of bush-pigs was crossing the fairway. As in the cow-killing episode, the ball was powerfully struck but a trifle low. The bush-pig is an unattractive animal which patrols the jungle with its tail stuck straight up in the air revealing a none-too-pleasant orifice underneath. Price's ball struck the lead bush-pig  in precisely that spot and stayed there, sending the animal rushing into the undergrowth squealing like, well, a stuck pig of course.

Golfers and geese do not, it seems, have a happy relationship. In Massachusetts a goose, having been struck by a golf ball which then came to rest by a water hazard, waddled over to the ball and kicked it into the water.

Then there was the

Case of the Murdered Goose.
A 67-year-old American, Dr Sherman Thomas, narrowly escaped going to jail for beating a Canadian Goose to death with his putter (evidence does not reveal whether it was a goose-neck putter). The assault took place on the 17th green at the fashionable Congressional Club in Washington. The doctor claimed in court that his approach shot struck the bird and, to put it out of its misery, he administered the *coup de grace*. Other evidence submitted stated that the doctor had attacked the bird because the creature had put him off with its mournful honking cry. The doctor's lawyers successfully applied for a 'plea bargain' and their client was fined $500 under the Migratory Birds Treaty Act.

BIZARRE
SUDDEN - DEATH
RECORDS

HEAVIEST DEFEAT

In the 1929 US Open at Winged Foot, Bobby Jones held a commanding lead during the final round but then frittered strokes away, finally holing a putt of twelve feet on the last green for a 79 to tie with Al Espinosa. The play-off over 36 holes was delayed so that Espinosa, a Roman Catholic, could attend Mass. Jones then administered the Last Rites to Espinosa's title hopes by handing out the heaviest play-off defeat on record – 141 to 164.

BIGGEST BOUNCE-BACK

In the 1976 Memorial Tournament, Roger Maltbie and Hale Irwin played sudden-death for the title. At the third extra hole, Maltbie's 4-iron second shot was hooking to perdition when the ball struck a gallery rope stake and bounced back onto the green. The hole was halved but on the next hole Irwin, no doubt somewhat miffed by his opponent's good fortune, drove behind a tree and lost the title. Irwin's golfing ledger was balanced, however, by the events of the 1984 Crosby Tournament at Pebble Beach when his drive to the 72nd hole was heading for the Pacific when it struck a rock and bounced back onto the fairway. Irwin was thus able to finish in a tie with Canadian Jim Nelford and he won the play-off.

WORST PLAY-OFF RECORD

Until recent times, the outcome of the four major championships was decided over a full 18-hole play-off and before that, over 36 holes. American Craig Wood is the only man to lose a play-off in each of the major championships. He lost the 1933 Open Championship at St Andrews to Densmore Shute, the 1934 US PGA to Paul Runyan, the 1935 US Masters to Gene Sarazen and the 1939 US Open in a play-off with Shute and Byron Nelson. In the 1935 Masters, Wood was tied by Sarazen when the latter holed a 4-wood second shot for an albatross on the 15th (see 'Shots Heard Around the World') and in his 1939 play-off Nelson holed his second shot at the 4th hole on his way to victory by three strokes. Wood did, however, win both the US Masters and US Open in 1941 – without the need of a play-off.

LONGEST AND MOST INCONCLUSIVE PLAY-OFF

Among the many forms of torture inflicted by the game, the sudden-death play-off provides perhaps the most exquisite pain. If, after 72 holes of gruelling stroke-play, two or more players are tied then the outcome has to be decided in the space of maybe no more than one hole. These play-offs only have relevance in major tournaments where they have been devised to bring proceedings to a swift conclusion and find a winner on the day. Neither of these requirements was in evidence in the 1949 Motor City Open when Cary Middlecoff and Lloyd Mangrum tied for first place. They battled through eleven extra holes without a result and eventually had to give way to darkness. They were declared joint winners.

Similar indecisiveness was demonstrated by Peter Thomson and Graham Marsh when they tied for first place in a Japanese tournament. The play-off was designated to be held over two particular holes and Thomson and Marsh went round both of them seven times before Thomson finally won the fourteenth hole.

After that, it hardly seems worth mentioning that in the 1973 Transvaal Open John Fourie beat Alan Henning at the ninth extra hole of a sudden-death play-off or that Johnny Miller took the same number of extra holes to see off Severiano Ballesteros in the 1981 Million Dollar Challenge.

MOST PROTRACTED PLAY-OFF

This took place in the 1974 World Series between Lee Trevino and Gary Player. Player's record in these showdowns is lamentable considering his reputation as a competitor, but on this occasion he stayed with Trevino for five extra holes before darkness prevailed. The next morning Player survived two more holes before adding another loss to his record.

LONGEST WINNING PUTT

The longest putt to win a sudden-death play-off was one of 85 feet holed by Bruce Lietzke to defeat Gene Littler in the 1977 Tucson Open.

LONGEST TIE

In the 1931 US Open at Inverness, George von Elm and Billy Burke tied after 72 holes on 292. After a 36-hole replay they were still tied at 149. Another 36 holes ensued before Burke finally won by 148 to 149. This is a record tie for a national Open championship.

STRANGEST CONCESSIONS

On occasions, players have become confused as to the actual format of a stroke-play play-off. The 1911 Open Championship at Royal St George's had a play-off between Harry Vardon and the Frenchman Arnaud Massy. Massy picked up his ball on the 35th hole after taking 148 strokes for 34 holes while Vardon had scored 143 for 35 holes. Thus Massy became the only player to concede a major stroke-play title prior to full completion.

Arnold Palmer was similarly confused in his play-off with Jack Nicklaus for the 1962 US Open at Oakmont. On the final green, Palmer conceded Nicklaus's final putt by tossing the ball back to him. Nicklaus was three strokes ahead at the time but, as it was stroke-play, he had to hole out. The ball was replaced and Nicklaus holed his final putt.

DRAMATIC
TURNAROUNDS

Counting chickens before they are hatched is a pastime in which, regardless of the mass of historical precedents, golfers continually indulge. There is scarcely a golfer anywhere who has not thought, at one time or another, that he or she had only to play the last three holes in level fives to win the monthly medal, or, when three up with four holes to play in a match, had only to get a couple of halves before the opponent would concede. The key-word in this psychological con-trick is **'only'** for its Siren-song has lured thousands of golfers onto the rocks of disaster, humiliation and degradation. Whenever that little word creeps into a golfer's subconscious then the subsequent fall from grace can be spectacularly awful.

In any collection of harrowing tales concerning defeat snatched from the jaws of victory, top spot in the horror catalogue would, in most people's opinion, go to the late Tony Lema. Champagne Tony was a playboy of the Western golfing world, a man with a supremely elegant swing and a similarly elegant attitude to life. In 1964 he achieved the almost unheard-of feat of winning the Open Championship at St Andrews with barely a full practice round over the Old Course. In 1965, as a result of this and other victories, Lema was invited to play in the World Match-Play Championship at Wentworth. He cruised through to the semi-finals where he faced Gary Player. The contrast between the two was stark. There was Lema, languid, debonair and sophisticated with a Latin air of indolence while Player, dressed all in black, was intense and brooding.

The morning round of this fateful encounter saw Lema round in an effortless 67 and six up at lunch. This meant that **he had only to produce steady golf in the afternoon** to be back in the clubhouse for tea. Lema won the first hole of the afternoon round to go seven up and the crowd drifted away, seeking other matches. The crowd's judgment appeared correct as Lema still stood five up with nine holes to play. Then Player won the 10th and 11th and suddenly Lema found a few doubts gnawing at him. They halved the 12th and then Lema hooked his tee shot at the 13th into the trees; he hacked out, knocked his third onto the green and holed a long putt for the four. His relief at this escape was short-lived as Player jammed home a putt for another win. By now Lema could sense he was a passenger in a juggernaut which was careering down a hill without any brakes; his wheels came off again at the 16th when he hooked into the trees to stand only one up.

News travels fast on a golf course and when the players arrived at the 17th, or 35th hole, the crowd had swelled enormously to witness the final act of the drama. The 17th hole was halved in birdie fours with Lema holing from around twelve feet and Player following him in from eight feet. Both men hit good drives up the 18th with Lema first to play the second shot. His reponse was the classic reflex action of a man in distress, he hooked the shot left and short of the green. Player lunged into his shot, the ball flew alarmingly near the trees on the right-hand edge of the green but at the last minute curved gently back on line to roll up ten feet from the flagstick. Lema's chip was well short of the hole and, with two putts, Player had drawn level. Lema was shattered and had no answer to Player's solid par four at the 37th.

It wasn't always champagne for Tony Lema, as the 1965 World Match-Play was to prove.

In the 1969 Alcan tournament at Portland, Oregon, Lee Trevino eagled the 15th hole to establish a six-stroke lead over his nearest rival, Billy Casper. **He had only to complete the formalities of the last three holes** to pick up a handsome cheque for $55,000. Trevino dropped a stroke at the 16th, and then on the par-three 17th bunkered his tee shot, took two to get out and then three-putted for a six. He parred the last hole but Casper, a man who made a habit of cashing in other players' misfortunes, had finished 3,2,3 to Trevino's 5,6,4 to win all the marbles.

More than any other form of competition, match-play provides a **rich source of chicken counting.** In a match at the Army GC, Aldershot in 1974, M. Smart was eight down with eight holes to play against M. Cook. In knockout match-play there is no such thing as being dormie, but Cook could have been forgiven for thinking he would soon be back in the clubhouse celebrating his victory. Nine holes later he was back in the clubhouse – but as the loser. Smart won the eight holes back and then the match at the 19th.

A glance at the records for the 1930 Walker Cup at Royal St George's would reveal that in the singles D. Moe of the USA defeated J. Stout of GB&I by one hole. This prosaic reference to yet another American victory does not do justice to one of the most remarkable turnarounds in Walker Cup history. In those days, the matches were over 36 holes, and at lunch Stout was four up on the American. Fortified by the meal, Stout began the afternoon round with three consecutive threes to go seven up. He was still seven up with thirteen holes to play but Moe, who eventually went round in 67, won back seven holes to draw level on the 35th green. On the final hole, Moe hit his second shot to within three feet of the hole to win the match.

The most dogged fight-back by the British in the Walker Cup occurred in the 1936 encounter at Pine Valley. In the first-day foursomes, George Voigt and Harry Girvan of the home side were seven up with eleven holes to play against the visiting pairing of Alec Hill and Cecil Ewing. By the 17th hole, the British were level and the last hole was halved.

The development of a killer instinct is regarded as of prime importance if a golfer is going to challange for the highest honours. **Kicking a man when he is down** was obviously alien to Al Watrous when he stood nine up on Bobby Cruickshank after 24 holes in a match in the 1932 US PGA Championship. On that 24th green, Watrous had conceded his opponent a putt of six feet for the half. And why not? After all, he had only to hang on for a few more holes to win and Bobby was a nice fellow who didn't deserve to be totally humiliated. But Watrous was an ill-fated golfer (see 'Shots Heard Around the World') and the fates hadn't finished with him. Cruickshank took his reprieve and started nibbling away at the deficit. By the time they reached the last hole, Watrous was only one up and Cruickshank squared the match with a long putt. On they went into extra holes and the humiliation was heaped upon Watrous when he lost at the 41st.

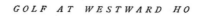

ON THE WAY—LATE AGAIN!

HAPPY THOUGHT!

UNHAPPY RESULT!

THE VICTORIOUS COUPLE

Examples of **profligate squandering in stroke-play** are legion. In the 1920 Open Championship at Royal Cinque Ports, Abe Mitchell was thirteen strokes ahead of the eventual winner, George Duncan, after two rounds. In the third round, Mitchell took 84 to Duncan's 71, thereby losing all thirteen strokes. Mitchell's raw Deal (sic) continued when Duncan added a 72 in the final round and Mitchell didn't even finish runner-up.

Probably the most condensed turnaround in a major championship occurred in the 1937 US Masters. Ralph Guldahl went into the final round four strokes ahead and maintained that position as he came to the short 12th. This particular hole, part of Augusta National's famous 'Amen Corner', is the most treacherous par three in championship golf. Guldahl added to that reputation by taking a five on it and then compounded the error by taking six at the 13th. Just ahead of him, Byron Nelson played the same two holes in 2,3 thereby making up six strokes which gave him a two-stroke victory.

Dropping down an echelon or two in terms of tournament prestige, let us take a look at Jim Hopper trying to qualify for the 1976 Californian Amateur Championship at Pebble Beach. Young Jim was one of those flippy-wristed kids who don't know the meaning of fear on a golf course and he cruised through 17 holes to have 14 strokes in hand to make the qualifying score. He had to play the 18th of course, but even this most daunting of par fives with the Pacific Ocean on the left and more out-of-bounds on the right should present no problem. **He had only to knock an iron down the middle** and two more safe iron shots would see him safely home. This was no time to pussy-foot around with an iron, thought Jim, let's give it the works with the driver. The first drive was in the ocean, and the second and third were also headed for Hawaii. Swivelling the gun a little to starboard he proceeded to hit two more drives out-of-bounds on the right. He failed to qualify by two shots.

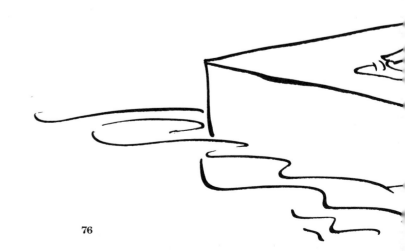

The fortunes of American professional Jack Renner took a dramatic turn for the worse in the 1983 Hawaii Open. Renner had finished his final round and was checking his card with Japan's Isao Aoki, still out on the course, the only man who could catch him. Aoki needed an eagle three on the last hole to win and was well short of the green in two strokes. Renner heard a tremendous roar from the course and thought Aoki had birdied the hole to tie. He hadn't. He'd **holed a 90-yard pitch shot to win** and become the first victorious Japanese golfer on the US Tour. Renner's happy ending came the following year when he took the title in Hawaii.

The record for the greatest disparity in scoring between two rounds in a single day is held by a professional, Don Hibbitts. In the pre-qualifying for the 1973 US Open he was round in 91 in the morning but improved by 23 strokes in the afternoon with a 68.

But let us end this chronicle of suffering with a message of hope. Dramatic turnarounds can sometimes work the other way, as in the case of Barry Galt, a 12-handicapper from Tulsa, Oklahoma. Playing at Pine Valley, the notoriously rugged course in New Jersey, Galt reached the turn in 50 strokes. The next nine holes saw Galt put up two fingers to the gods of golfing malice. Turning for home, he birdied the next five holes, dropped a stroke at the 17th and **he had only to birdie the final hole** for a homeward half of 31. He did, to complete two halves which showed a difference of 19 strokes.

FEMININE FRAILTY

Golf historians are fairly unanimous that the first woman golfer of any note was Mary, Queen of Scots. Indeed, at her trial, prior to her execution in 1584, the prosecution made great play of the fact that, a few days after the death of her husband, Darnley, she was seen playing golf in the fields beside Seton. Mary, of course, **paid the extreme penalty for lifting her head** by having it removed. Unfortunately for subsequent generations of women golfers, her fate did not light a beacon for golfing emancipation – in fact, it could be said that the male-dominated golfing world is still somewhat disappointed that her comeuppance didn't start a trend.

       Proof of the enduring male chauvinism in the game is provided by the staging of a Ladies' Stableford Competition at Royal St George's in 1976. Nothing unusual in that, you might think, except for the fact that it was the first time in the club's 89-year history that a women's competition had been held there. The women had to play off the men's tees since at Royal St George's these are the only tees in existence.

       In recent years women's golf has made great strides, with prize-money for lady professionals scaling new heights. Women are no less prone to disaster than men and also compete just as fiercely. Lady golf writer Lewine Mair

JoAnne Carner tries to see her way out of a tight spot.

recounts the story of when she was playing a match against another lady, and as the round progressed, Lewine was holing putts from everywhere. As another long putt dropped, Lewine's opponent turned to her and said:

'If you do that once more **I shall slap your face.**'

30. — NEW WOMAN.

Whenever victory, prestige and money are at stake, the fates do not discriminate between the sexes. While the tragedy of Roberto de Vicenzo in the 1968 US Masters (see 'Bizarre Championship Records') has passed into the annals of the game, an even worse tragedy befell the Hawaiian golfer Jackie Pung in the 1957 US Women's Open. Mrs Pung completed her final round and would have won had she not signed for an incorrect scorecard.

One hole was marked for a five when in fact she took six although her final round total was correct. She was disqualified, but friends made a collection for her afterwards of $3,000 which was more than the first prize.

Consider too the case of Japanese professional Tatsuko Ohsako, playing in the 1982 American Express Sun City Classic on the US LPGA Tour. Miss Ohsako had played 56 holes of the tournament without a bogey and was leading comfortably. On the third hole of her final round she drove behind a tree, her second shot ricocheted off the tree and hit her club for an automatic two-stroke penalty. She finished the hole with a four-over-par eight and with a double-bogey at the 17th she finished in a tie for sixth place, four strokes behind the winner.

In the second round of the Inamori Classic, American professional LeAnn Cassaday had six consecutive birdies from the 5th hole. On the 11th she took a five over par nine. 'It didn't really bother me,' said Miss Cassaday afterwards, 'what did bother me was adding it all up.'

High scores are not, of course, the sole preserve of the professionals. An American lady amateur playing in a competition at Preakness Hills GC, New Jersey in 1973 came to the short 18th with a handy twenty-three stroke lead over the rest of the field. It was not enough. **She put fourteen shots into a lake** in front of the green and lost.

The world record for the highest score on one hole is held by an anonymous American lady amateur. Playing in a women's qualifying competition in 1912 at the Shawnee Country Club, this intrepid competitor knew that the number of entrants was the same as the number of qualifying places so all she had to do was complete the round. On the 16th hole she plonked her tee shot into a stream in front of the green. Since she was playing with a 'floater' she could see her errant missile bobbing about in the waves. Not wishing to abandon her ball and determined to complete her round, she commandeered a nearby boat and summoned her husband to get in and start rowing. On arriving at the ball she lashed at it sending up a shower of water which soaked her and her long-suffering husband. Cruising gently downstream, she lashed and she splashed until finally she made contact. The ball flew out of the water and sought sanctuary in the woods. But there was no place to hide from this particular golfer. The ball was located by the dripping couple and eventually **hacked onto the green and into the hole on the 166th stroke.**

On occasions, the scorn heaped upon women golfers by their male counterparts does appear to have some justification. One inevitable criticism is that women golfers talk too much on the course and don't get on with the game. Tomiko Yamashita and her cousin did the cause of women's golf no good at all when playing the sixth hole of a course in Hawaii. Chattering together they approached the green when, to their consternation, neither of them could find their respective golf balls. Finally the reason occurred to them. They had forgotten to drive off.

Lady drivers of golf balls are treated with much the same derision as lady drivers of motor cars. In the 1975 Walker Cup at St Andrews, the two were neatly juxtaposed when a car driven by **an elderly District Nurse** ventured onto the Old Course. Suddenly it dawned on the driver that she was in the wrong place at the wrong time as the crowds seethed about the course. Rather in the manner of a rabbit caught in the headlights of a car, she turned this way and that, finding that each escape route was blocked. In desperation she made a final dash for safety and drove straight into a pot bunker – placed there for the express

Trapped! The district nurse at St Andrews in 1975.

purpose of catching errant drives.

Starting them young is an old adage, but in the case of American Beverly Klass it was taken to ridiculous lengths. At the age of eight she won the National Pee-Wee title by 65 strokes and a year later, encouraged by her father, she turned professional. By 1967, at the age of 11, she was playing the US LPGA Tour where she had a stroke average of 90 and won over $100. She suffered mentally from the experience during her teens and returned to the amateur ranks before turning pro again at the age of 19.

The final round of the 1967 US Open (male) saw Arnold Palmer and Jack Nicklaus paired together, accompanied by a huge gallery. As the match passed through the 4th hole at Baltusrol, it was decided to move a group of portable lavatories across to the 16th to accommodate the returning crowd. As one of the privvies was lifted onto a lorry, **a loud scream emanated from within** and the door flew open to reveal a partly clad lady who didn't stop screaming until she reached the trees.

Early in 1982 a story spread like wildfire through the American newspapers and magazines concerning the golfing prowess of Princess Diana. The report stated that while playing a friendly four-ball at Royal Troon with Prince Charles, Princess Anne and Prince Andrew, **the Princess had holed in one at the 8th,** the famous Postage Stamp. Further investigations revealed that the story was a hoax and drew the comment from the beleaguered Buckingham Palace Press Office that: 'It was probably dreamed up by some fool with a typewriter.'

In a women's professional tournament at Mere, Cheshire in 1982, Joanna Smurthwaite was bunkered by the 16th green in two shots. She splashed out to six feet but missed the tricky downhill putt for her par four. In exasperation she kicked her putter which came out of her hands, slid across the green and struck her ball. Jo watched in agony as her ball began gathering pace down the green, finally coming to rest in the bunker she had recently vacated. She played the ball back onto the green and two-putted, marking her score as eight which included one penalty stroke. Recording the incident later to an official, she was told she should have replaced the ball in the position it was in before it was struck by the putter, adding one stroke to her score to give herself a six. Since she had not observed the Rules of Golf and played the ball from the bunker, she should have

The formidable Leitch sisters at Turnberry in 1912. Standing, left to right: Miss Peggy, Miss Cecil. Seated: Miss Chris, Miss Edith, Miss May.

added two penalty strokes to the eight and signed her card for a ten. The only recourse which could be taken was disqualification since she had signed her card for a score which was lower than it should have been.

Supreme concentration in the face of family crisis was shown by an American mother of seven who started a round and played six holes before she received a message to pick up one of her daughters who had broken her foot. The mother made the pick-up and then returned to the 7th hole and finished the first nine holes. At the 10th there was another message concerning another daughter who was in the principal's office at her school having been caught in possession of some marijuana. Mother collected the erring offspring and returned once more to her round. She played a further five holes when the message came through that yet another daughter had to be collected from school owing to an outbreak of measles in the class. Mother took the child home and put her to bed. She completed her round by birdieing the last two holes to win the tournament and then had to rush from the course to pick up her son who had just been fired from his job. In our opinion she should have been disqualified from the tournament for persistent breach of Rule 37-7: 'The player shall at all times play without undue delay.'

Playing at the Smithers GC in British Columbia, Lane Johnson's tee shot sent her ball towards the woods. The ball struck a tree, bounced straight back and **lodged in her bra.**

Let us not end this discussion on feminine frailty without recognizing that women do have their place on a golf course, although sometimes their presence is accompanied by the proverbial nudge and wink. In the 1984 English Amateur Championship at Woodhall Spa, one player's girl friend wore the briefest pair of shorts ever witnessed on a golf course. As elderly male officials persistently wiped the steam from their glasses, it was suggested that the lady in question be deemed a 'Movable Distraction' as an addendum to Rule 31-1.

Perhaps it is appropriate that the last word on women's role in golf should come from the Royal & Ancient Golf Club of St Andrews. For centuries women have been barred from entering the hallowed portals of the clubhouse but an historic moment seemed nigh when, during a ladies' championship, a group of women huddled in the lee of the clubhouse, sheltering from a storm. Suddenly they spied the steward from the R & A walking towards them. Could this be it, they thought? Finally **the bigots within were going to relent** and allow them inside to shelter?

'Ladies,' said the steward, 'I have a message for you.'

The ladies waited with baited breath, not wishing to miss one syllable of this declaration of peace in the battle of the sexes.

'The members request,' continued the steward, 'that you do not shelter in front of the window, you are obscuring the view.'

MOST INEFFECTIVE BURST OF LOW SCORING
In the 1978 Swiss Open at Crans-sur-Sierre, Spanish professional Jose-Maria Canizares embarked on a remarkable run of scoring. In the second round he birdied each of the last five holes for a round of 67 and then began his third round with six consecutive birdies, breaking the sequence with an eagle at the 7th. He was out in 27, which tied the world record, and finished with a 64. His last round was 10 strokes worse and he finished four strokes behind the winner, Severiano Ballesteros, who was the model of consistency with four rounds of 68 apiece.

MOST TRIVIAL GOLFING INFORMATION
Some items of intense interest were revealed when Dan Stahl gave up playing golf at the age of 85 having been a stalwart of the Pasadena Club in St Petersburg for 27 years. Throughout this period he kept a diary which revealed the following statistics. He played 4,890 rounds of golf, lost 1,638 balls, paid $7,387 in green fees and wore out nine golf bags and six trolleys. Among the miscellaneous items he noted were that he fed the birds on the course no less than 1,400 loaves of bread, and killed 126 snakes. Proof that Florida is indeed the Sunshine State was indicated by the fact that he only suffered rain on 52 occasions in his near 5,000 outings.

MOST PERSISTENT QUALIFIER
American Mac O'Grady made 16 attempts to gain his US Tour card before succeeding with No 17 in the November 1982 Qualifying School.

LONGEST SHORT HOLE
The 9th hole at Portal GC measures only 125 yards but most people take about 65 minutes to play it. The reason? The tee is in North Portal, Saskatchewan, Canada while the green is in Portal, North Dakota, USA. North Dakota observes daylight saving time but its Canadian neighbour does not and is therefore an hour ahead. This makes it the longest short hole in the world in terms of playing time.

LONGEST CROSS-COUNTRY ROUND
Floyd Rood played from coast to coast across the United States from 14 September 1963 to 3 October 1964. He took 114,737 strokes and lost 3,511 balls on the 3,397.7 mile journey.

MOST PERIPATETIC GOLFER
American Ralph Kennedy played on 3,615 courses up to his death in 1962 at the age of 80. Each of his scorecards was attested by an official of the club and he played in every State in the United States, every Province in Canada and twelve other countries. He played his 3,000th round over the Old Course at St Andrews. Not attested are the 5,000-plus courses alleged to have been played by Australian- born Joe Kirkwood, a noted trick-shot artist between the Wars.

HIGHEST AVERAGE
In 1888, Chevalier von Sittern completed 18 holes at Biarritz in 316 strokes, an average of 17.55 strokes per hole.

LEAST PRIZE-MONEY
In his first year on the US Tour, 1969, professional Bob Watson won a total of $1.88 in prize-money.

HIGHEST OPEN PRE-QUALIFYING SCORE (1)

When an entry for the 1965 Open Championship was received from Walter Danecki of Milwaukee, who described himself as a professional, his name went straight into the draw for the qualifying rounds. Danecki was, in fact, a mail sorter whose golf experience was limited to a few rounds on a local municipal course, but since he was after the money which would come from his victory at Royal Birkdale his conscience directed that he put the word 'professional' down on his entry form. His performance in the first qualifying round at Hillside soon gave the lie to his description – Walter was round in a spirited 108 strokes. The Royal & Ancient officials were somewhat perplexed at what to do next since Danecki was entitled to his second attempt and Walter refused to quit, saying that he liked to play golf and that's what he was jolly well going to do. The officials retired with as much good grace as they could muster and Walter put in another storming score, this time of 113. As the Press gathered round our hero, he put his attitude right in perspective. 'I'm glad I played your small ball,' said Walter, 'if I'd played the big ball I'd have been all over the place.' He failed to qualify for the Open Championship by 75 strokes.

Walter Danecki en route to 113 at Royal Birkdale, 1965.

LONGEST REBOUND (HEADED)

In September 1913 at the Machrie course on the Isle of Arran, a ball rebounded from the head of a caddie a distance of 42 yards 2 feet 10 inches, the distance being measured by three people as witnesses. In the same month of the same year Edward Sladward, playing at the Premier Mine course in South Africa, struck his caddie on the head, the ball rebounding in a direct line a distance of 75 yards. This remains the unofficial world record.

GREATEST DIFFERENCE IN SCORING BY GOLFER WITH UNPRONOUNCEABLE NAME

Before the recent introduction of zonal pre-qualifying, the World Cup attracted entries from many countries where golf was still in its infancy. In the 1979 event at Glyfada, Athens, a Fijiian player rejoicing in the name of Bose Lutunatabua recorded a second-round score of 92. In the final round he took 71, a difference of 21 strokes.

MOST AMAZING ROUND

In the 1936 Italian Open Championship at Sestrieres, near Turin, American professional Joe Ezar had a third round score of 64 in which he had nominated his score on each hole beforehand. Prior to the round, Ezar struck a bet with the club president that he would do a 64 and then jotted down on a piece of paper his score on each hole. Ezar kept to his schedule throughout the round, apparently holing a 50-yard pitch shot on the 9th hole to gain his nominated three there. He was out in 32 and home in the same score to complete the most amazing round in the history of the game.

HIGHEST OPEN PRE-QUALIFYING SCORE (2)

Following the Danecki episode, the R & A took steps to screen all entrants for the Open Championship. Eleven years later, however, the security had become a little lax and an entry from 'professional' Maurice Flitcroft slipped through the net. Flitcroft was in fact a crane-driver from Barrow-in-Furness whose golf experience was even more limited than Danecki's – he had only taken up the game some 18 months previously and had practised on a local playing field, using a children's sand-pit for bunker play. When Flitcroft teed off at Formby in the first qualifying round for the 1976 Open Championship, it was the first 18 holes of his life. Maurice raced to the turn in 61 strokes, give or take a few which escaped his marker, but pulled himself together on the inward half with a 60 – total 121.

'I've made a lot of progress in the last few months,' said Maurice in his post-round interview, 'but I was trying too hard at the beginning. I began to put things together at the end of the round.'

The R & A were spared further embarrassment when Flitcroft withdrew from the Championship, but not before announcing, like General MacArthur, that he would return.

HIGHEST OPEN PRE- QUALIFYING SCORE (2½)

Following the Flitcroft fiasco, the R & A took even greater steps to screen entrants for the Open Championship. In the first qualifying round for the 1983 Championship, held at Pleasington, competitor Gerald Hoppy from Switzerland scored 63. Unfortunately for Gerald, this was for the first nine holes. Officials, smelling a pungent rat, rushed to the scene and turfed Gerald off the course. Gerald was none other than the same Flitcroft who had entered under an assumed name and from a different country. He had made good his vow to return.

MOST FREQUENT RUNNER-UP (PROFESSIONAL)

Australian professional Wayne Grady was runner-up in 17 tournaments before finally winning the 1984 German Open.

LONGEST OCCUPANCY OF CLUBHOUSE BAR

After a round of golf in the Tropics it is vital to replace the fluids which have drained away in the heat of the midday sun. In Kenya, this activity takes precedence over all others. In order not to speak ill of those who are no longer with us, let us refer to this particular record-holder as simply 'Harry'. Old Harry liked his round of golf at the Karen Country Club on the outskirts of Nairobi. He also liked the conviviality of the bar afterwards and he particularly liked the replacement of those vital body fluids. He liked them so much that when he died, a clause in his will requested that his ashes be taken aloft in an aeroplane and scattered over his beloved clubhouse; perhaps a few of them would drift into the bar where they would be perfectly at home. This request was duly carried out. The following week the entire clubhouse, including Harry's remains, was burnt to the ground.

GET ME
TO THE
TEE
on
TIME

It's in the Rules. Rule 37-5, to be precise: 'The player shall start at the time and in the order arranged by the Committee. Penalty for breach of rule – Disqualification.'

Time and the official starter wait for no man, or woman for that matter. The incidence of players missing their tee-off times in important tournaments is extraordinarily high. Most famously in recent times was the case of Severiano Ballesteros in the 1980 US Open at Baltusrol. After a disappointing first round of 75, which left him 12 strokes behind the leaders, Jack Nicklaus (the eventual winner) and Tom Weiskopf, Ballesteros left his hotel for the second round in a chauffeur-driven car. The traffic was heavy and when the car finally arrived at the course, the Spaniard was told he was due on the tee. He rushed to the locker-room and changed his shoes **but he was seven minutes late.** Rule 37-5 was applied and Ballesteros was out of the Championship.

Perhaps Ballesteros should have taken a leaf out of Gary Player's book when the South African found himself similarly held up in traffic while trying to get to a course. He hitched a ride on the back of a motor-bike.

One can only sympathize with the competitor from Burma who, in the days before inter-Continental jet travel, entered the 1937 British Amateur Championship at Royal St George's. This intrepid traveller set off by ship across the Pacific to San Francisco. From there he caught a train to New York where he boarded the *Queen Mary* to cross the Atlantic. On arrival at Southampton, he took a car to Sandwich **and arrived four hours late** for his starting time!

The record for missing a tee-off time by the widest margin must surely go to James McDermott, the US Open champion of 1911 and 1912. He arrived to play in the 1914 Open Championship at Prestwick only to discover that **he was a week overdue.**

In the 1922 British Amateur Championship at Prestwick, a competitor boarded a train at Ayr thinking it stopped at the course. It didn't. The train ended its journey at Troon some miles further on. The railway runs alongside the first hole at Prestwick and the competitor could be heard yelling frantically that he would be back as soon as he could. It wasn't soon enough and he was disqualified.

Three Open champions were involved in some narrow squeaks in their year of triumph. Before the start of the final two rounds in the 1936 Open at Hoylake the eventual winner, Alfred Padgham, discovered **his clubs were locked in a local clubmaker's shop** with his caddie nowhere to be seen. Padgham smashed a window, retrieved his clubs and hired a new caddie. Similarly, in 1952, Bobby Locke left his car containing his clubs in a lock-up garage near where he was staying for that year's Open at Royal Lytham & St Annes. When Locke arrived at the garage to collect his car to take him to the course for the final two rounds, the garage owner was nowhere to be seen. It was early in the morning so Locke hitched a ride in a passing milk-float and roused the slumbering garage-owner who opened up for the locked-out Locke.

In the 1981 Open at Royal St George's, American Bill Rogers was quietly practising on the putting-green when a passing journalist informed him he had about one minute to present himself on the first tee for the opening round. Rogers made it and went on to win the Championship.

In the 1940 US Open at Canterbury GC, Ohio no less than six players were disqualified for starting *before* their tee-off time. In those days, the final two rounds were played in one day and on this occasion, at lunch, Ed 'Porky' Oliver, 'Dutch' Harrison and Johnny Bulla were well placed with the afternoon round to play. A storm threatened the area and Oliver was keen to get on with the round so he and his partners set off twenty-eight minutes early. They were followed by the threesome of Ky Laffoon, Duke Gibson and Claude Harmon. All six were zapped by Rule 37-5 with Oliver, in particular, feeling the most aggrieved. His final round of 71 would have put him in a tie for first place.

American lady professional Connie Chillemi set her alarm clock to wake her in time for a round in a US LPGA tournament. The clock failed in its duty and Miss Chillemi dashed from her motel room, hair still in curlers, and jumped into her car. The 20-minute journey to the course took her 10 minutes as she touched speeds of 110 mph in a 55-mph speed zone. As she approached the course the police were in hot pursuit. In order to get into the course entrance, she had to cross the central reservation and the traffic travelling in the opposite direction. This she achieved without hitting anyone but the police got there first and with guns drawn ordered Miss Chillemi to 'freeze' as she reached for her player's card to prove her identity. By the time the facts had been established and a speeding ticket issued, **she had missed her starting time by two minutes.** She was eventually fined $500, and her other expenses for that nightmare morning included a new alarm clock.

At the Sea Pines Heritage Classic at Hilton Head Island in 1983,

young professional Jodie Mudd opened with a 66. During the second round there was a lengthy rain delay and play resumed with Mudd waiting on the 4th hole. What he was waiting for was his caddie and clubs. Both failed to appear so Mudd was disqualified for not being ready when play was due to restart.

On some occasions, the urgency with which players get to the course is not reflected in the time they take to get round. In the 1972 World Cup at Royal Melbourne GC, Australia, a four-ball containing Gary Player, representing South Africa, took six hours and 45 minutes to complete the course. No penalty was awarded, unlike the case of Benny Passons, playing in the 1979 North Texas PGA Championship. Mr Passons arrived on the 54th and final tee with a commanding three-stroke lead. Moments later his lead had shrunk to one as he was penalized two strokes under Rule 37-7: 'The player shall at all times play without undue delay.' He still won.

No officials were present at the Wailea course in Hawaii when a terrible delay developed. The club despatched somebody to go out and investigate. The source of the trouble turned out to be four Japanese golfers whose previous golf experience had been confined to the driving range. Apparently it was **the first time they had ever set foot on a proper golf course** and they had only brought four balls with them. After three of the balls had been lost, they overcame this difficultly by allowing one player to hit his shot, run forward to where the ball lay, mark the spot and return with the ball to his fellows for them to go through the same procedure.

Japanese professional Haruo Yasuda finished a 36-hole tournament in his homeland with a four under par total of 140. He decided he had no chance of victory as the leader, Keji Sogame, was still out on the course at eight under par. Yasuda took the next flight home only to arrive at his destination to find the result was a lot closer than he anticipated. Sogame had blown his lead and had finished tied with Yasuda. With no play-off possible, Sogame took the first prize of £7,500 while Yasuda had to be content with half that amount.

BIZARRE STROKES

MOST CONTIGUOUS BALLS

It was obviously going to be one of those days for young professional Philip Parkin as he began his second round in the 1984 Cannes Open at Mougins. Starting at the 10th, he three-putted and then followed this with four putts at the 12th. On the 14th his tee shot disappeared into a bush, and when the ball was located it was in an appalling lie. Parkin decided his only course of action was to shut his eyes and hit as hard as he could. He made good contact and opened his eyes just in time to see the ball dropping back into the place it had just left. Parkin hit the ball again and sent it on its way – much to the consternation of his playing companions who had seen the first ball emerge and run down the fairway. The second ball had been lying directly underneath the first and had popped up when the first was struck. The two-stroke penalty he incurred meant he finally holed out in seven.

J. Wilson was playing the 3rd hole at Stonehaven GC in 1924. Mr Wilson obviously had a built-in fault in his swing as, for the second week running, his tee shot finished in a ditch. As he struck the ball from the ditch another ball emerged at the same time. The second ball was the one he had lost the week previously in the same ditch.

QUICKEST ROUND

Playing in a competition at Sandwell Park GC, S. Cooper completed the course in one stroke. His opening drive finished in the hole on the 18th green. Similar economy was demonstrated by Eamonn Pointer playing the 15th hole at the Port Royal course in Bermuda. Driving into a howling wind, he caught his tee shot off the top of the club and although the ball tried valiantly to make forward progress, the elements proved too much. The ball flew back over the striker's shoulder, rolled onto the nearby 17th green and into the hole.

An enthusiastic blind golfer who only needed the clubhead aligned to play some excellent golf: Gerry Brereton preparing to chip at Caddington, Surrey.

Jose Maria Canizares's caddy supervises, from the television gantry, the Spaniard's efforts to retrieve the ball from a dead tree at Moor Park during the 1979 Tournament Players Championship.

MOST GOLF-STRUCK FATHER

Albertini Rodriguez from Spain was just eight months old when his father, a golf mad 6-handicap player, decided to have him baptized in the lake separating the tee and green on the par-three 6th hole on Quinta do Lago's 'C' course in the Algarve. The father was determined that his son would be a great golfer and intoned these solemn words to him at the christening:

'You have been in this water once but I never want to hear of you in it again when you play golf.'

While out playing the following day, the proud father failed to set his son any kind of example. At the same hole he put his tee shot in the water.

MOST REJUVENATED SHOT

Approaching the 16th green at Coombe Wood GC, a player hit his ball into the vertical exhaust of a tractor which was mowing the fairway. The greenkeeper was surprised to find a temporary loss of power in the vehicle but when sufficient compression had built up in the exhaust system, the ball rocketed out, bounced off the roof of a nearby house and landed some three feet from the hole.

MOST STIRRING RESCUE

In 1954, four anglers were fishing from an island which was caught in a rising flood. Three of the fishermen escaped to the mainland but the fourth was trapped. It was impossible to throw him a rope and the situation looked serious until the timely arrival on the scene of R. Murray, the Wigtownshire Amateur Champion. Like all sensible golfers, Mr Murray had his clubs with him because you never know when you might get a game. He calculated the distance to the island and reckoned it required a firm 8-iron to make the carry, allowing for the fact that first he had to drive a nail through the ball. He then attached a piece of string to the nail and hit the ball across the water to the marooned angler. The string was tied to a strong rope and this was hauled across by the angler who tied it to a tree and swung himself across the river to safety.

MOST BIZARRE RECOVERY SHOT

In the history of competitive golf there has probably never been a more unusual recovery shot than the one played by Nigel Denham in the 1974 Brabazon Trophy at Moortown GC, near Leeds. Denham's second shot to the 18th green was a little strong and a little long. Its final resting place was even longer than he could have imagined in his wildest dreams. The ball pitched on a path in front of the clubhouse, bounced up the steps through an open door and, as if anticipating its owner's post-round requirements, struck a wall and rebounded into the bar. The owner soon followed and, having removed his spikes, he consulted the local rules.

The clubhouse was not out-of-bounds and so it was clear that his ball lay within the confines of an immovable obstruction. His ball, however, was surrounded by a host of movable obstructions such as tables, chairs, beer mats and drinkers. These were moved so that Denham could follow the true traditions of the game and play the ball as it lay, in this case from a carpet. He had a clear line to the green through a closed window. Naturally, he opened the window to avoid any damage and played a crisp pitch through the aperture onto the green, some 12 feet from the hole. Later, the incident was referred to the Rules of Golf Committee at St Andrews which ruled that Denham should have been penalized two strokes for opening the window as it was an integral part of the immovable obstruction and, therefore, should not have been moved.

PS The clubhouse at Moortown is now out-of-bounds.

FIRST TIME I'VE SEEN HIM GET A ROUND IN .....

MOST ELEVATED GOLFERS

Whoever said that trees are 90 per cent air obviously never tried to hit a golf ball through one, but if there is any truth in that assessment it is remarkable how many times golf balls remain lodged in the 10 per cent. Usually, the wisest course of action is to take a penalty and drop another ball but sometimes circumstances dictate otherwise. In the third round of the 1981 Benson & Hedges International at Fulford GC, West Germany's Bernhard Langer gained world-wide fame when his second shot to the 17th lodged in a large tree to the left of the green. Langer clambered up into the branches and chipped the ball out onto the green from where he took two more putts. He eventually finished second in the tournament, one stroke behind the winner.

In the 1964 Australian Wills Masters, Arnold Palmer found himself literally up a gum tree when his second shot to the 9th hole lodged in a member of the species. Taking a 1-iron, Palmer climbed 20 feet up the tree and, reversing the head of the club, knocked the ball out towards the green and holed out in two more strokes.

At Crawfordville, Indiana in 1923, a Mrs Blackford hit her ball into a tree where it came to rest in a bird's nest. She too climbed up and played a brilliant pitch onto the green and holed the putt to halve the hole.

LONGEST ALBATROSS

An albatross (three under par) is a pretty rare golfing bird requiring two long and accurate shots on a par-five hole. John Eakin of California recorded the longest known albatross when he holed his second shot at the 609-yard 15th hole at the Makaha Inn course in Hawaii in 1972.

TOUGHEST COURSE

Many courses lay claim to be the toughest in the world and in any list of this type there is no doubt that Pine Valley on the New Jersey side of Philadelphia would be somewhere near the top. Carved out of a pine forest, each hole provides the golfer with a tee, a patch of fairway and a green while in between there is nothing but sand, scrub and perdition. The course is really one huge 184-acre bunker with a few patches of grass in selected places.

Woody Platt, a good local amateur, started one round with a birdie three and began to feel good. He felt even better when on the 367-yard 2nd he holed his second shot for an eagle two. Nirvana was just around the corner when, on the 3rd, he holed-in-one and followed this with another birdie on the 461-yard 4th. He was now six under par after four holes on some of the roughest golfing terrain in the world. The first four holes at Pine Valley make a full circle back to the clubhouse. If ever there was a time for a quick snort of the old tincture, if only to brace the spirits for the ordeal of the short 5th, this was it. Platt duly repaired to the clubhouse. He never came out to complete the round.

Bernhard Langer and his famous tree recovery in the 1981 Benson & Hedges International.

A. Moir receives advice on club selection for his second shot at Wentworth's 10th hole.

HARDEST COURSE

In 1939 a bet was struck that Richard Sutton, a London stockbroker, could not play from Tower Bridge to White's Club in St James's Street in under 200 strokes. Using a putter, Sutton crossed the Thames at Southwark Bridge and, hitting the ball short distances to avoid trouble, completed the 'course' in 142 strokes to win the bet.

MOST CONSISTENT ROUNDS

In a tournament round at Royal Ashdown Forest in 1936 Bobby Locke, then an amateur, completed each hole in four strokes for a 72. This feat was also achieved in the days of hickory shafts and the guttie ball by Ben Sayers who did it for a bet at Royal Burgess.

MOST NUMERATE START

At Torfin GC, near Edinburgh in 1920, William Ingle began his round 1-2-3-4-5. And at Hidden Valley GC, Oregon a group of players scored 1-2-3-4-5-6 at the par-three 7th.

MOST THRIFTY WIFE

Playing the 6th hole at the Live Oak course in Texas, G. Hamilton hit his second shot into a tree near the green. The ball did not emerge and Hamilton abandoned it as lost. Realizing that golf balls cost good money, Mrs Hamilton was playing the same hole four weeks later when she remembered her husband's lost ball. She then struck her second shot into the same tree. Her ball reappeared along with her husband's missing ball.

MOST SUNKEN GOLFER

When burly 14-stone D. J. Bayly MacArthur knocked his ball into a bunker at the Rose Bay course in New South Wales during a round in 1931 his chief concern was what sort of lie he would find in the hazard. On reaching his ball he took a club and stepped boldly into the sand. He wriggled his feet a little to secure his stance and then slowly he began to sink. He had stepped on a patch of quicksand and had sunk up to his armpits before his cries for help were heard and he was rescued.

MOST INTIMATE DRIVE

Playing the 10th hole at the Iron Temple Country Club in Pennsylvania, Richard Bachman caught his tee shot a little low. The ball struck the ladies' tee marker and caromed off towards the club swimming pool where it struck the diving-board and landed on the bikini-clad posterior of a lady sunbather. Mr Bachman's embarrassment was slightly relieved by the fact that the recipient of this golf-ball goosing was **none other than his wife.**

WARTIME GOLF

ER, JUST GETTING OUR BALL BACK

During the First World War golf was attempted by British POWs in a prison camp, but with nothing like the same ingenuity displayed by the residents of Stalag Luft III in the Second World War. The circumstances have been beautifully recorded for the simple reason that the late Pat Ward-Thomas, for nearly thirty years the golf correspondent of *The Guardian*, was a prisoner there for almost five years and was one of the founder members of the Sagan Golf Club as it came to be known.

In the early days at the camp all kinds of games were played such as cricket, soccer and rugby but the most significant sporting event occurred the day one of the inmates received a hickory-shafted lady's mashie. The arrival of this club **sparked off a frenzy of ball-making** in which anything made of, or containing, rubber was commandeered for use in the centre of the ball while the covers were made of leather, obtained by cutting shoes into pieces, which were cut into strips and sewn together. An example of one of these balls is now in the Royal and Ancient Museum in St Andrews and its weight and size are precisely the same as a real ball (1.62 inches: 1.62 ounces).

The next requirement was a course. In such a confined space this might have seemed impossible but no, a nine-hole layout was constructed providing many testing shots, measuring a total of 850 yards with a par of 29. Greens were made by clearing an area of stones and roots and covering the levelled ground with yellow sand. Upkeep of the greens became difficult after the famous 'Wooden Horse' escape from the camp and the excavation of yellow sand was *verboten*; in its place the golfers used black sand which lay nearer the surface.

The boundaries of the course were clearly defined by the barbed-wire perimeter fence which was not only out-of-bounds for the balls but also for the striker. Dispensation was given, however, for players to retrieve balls which crossed into the no-man's land between the outer wire and the internal trip-wire.

Being the only club in the camp for some time (more clubs did arrive later), the little lady's mashie had to serve all players but the competitive spirit was no less intense. Those people who came to know Pat Ward-Thomas later in life were soon made aware of his intolerance of his own failings, as on the occasion when he had topped three successive fairway wood shots and then grasped the offending club in both hands saying:

'If you do that once more I shall break your bloody neck!'

The explosive nature of his temperament was also in evidence in Stalag Luft III. While playing there with Oliver Green, later to become the supremo at Woburn Golf & Country Club, Pat struck an imperfect stroke and in his fury **sent the camp club whirling in the air,** the implement making a noise like a startled partridge. As soon as the club left his hands he realized the enormity of his action and clutched despairingly after it. It was too late – the club flew over the perimeter wire and it was some time before it was retrieved.

Prison golf of an entirely different nature took place during the Vietnam conflict. For seven years, George Hall of Hattiesburg, Missouri was a POW of the VietCong. During that time, although confined to a cell measuring seven feet square, he played a round of golf every day. Hall visualized the course he was playing and used a stick for a club. He would hit his drive and then **pace off 240 yards round the cell** before deciding on his second shot and repeating the process. In his mental rounds Hall would only score pars, no birdies or bogeys, and he would even imagine conversations he was having with his companions. At the end of his ordeal, Hall had golf to thank for keeping him sane.

'Bunker' practice for a US Marine in Lebanon.

In the Second World War golfing life still went on in dear old Blighty, although sometimes it was mildly inconvenienced by the Luftwaffe. Potential damage by bombs was clearly uppermost in the mind of Major G. L. Edsell, then Secretary of the St Mellon's GC in Monmouthshire, when he posted the following local rules on the notice board.

'During gunfire or while bombs are falling, players can take cover without penalty for slow play.

Players should pick up bomb or shell splinters from the fairways to save damage to mowers.

Position of known delayed-action bombs are marked by flags at a reasonable, but not guaranteed, safe distance.

Bomb splinters can be removed from greens, or elsewhere when within one club length. No penalty.

A ball moved by enemy action can be replaced at its original location. No penalty. If the ball is lost or destroyed, a free drop is allowed.

Free drop allowed for a ball resting in a bomb crater.

A player whose stroke is affected by the explosion of a bomb or by machine-gun fire may replay the shot under a penalty of one stroke.'

Bombs were probably responsible for a spectacular shot which took place at Killermont GC during the Second World War. Several missiles had landed in the Glasgow area and one of these may have loosened the roots of a magnificent beech tree which guarded the 5th green. One day, while playing the hole, a golfer sent his second shot straight at the tree which measured over five feet in diameter. As though it had taken all the punishment it could from errant approaches, the tree slowly toppled to the ground.

Similar problems were experienced at Weymouth GC where Fred Beets was the professional for many years. During his time at the club he served in every capacity, not only as professional but also as barman, secretary, cleaner and greenkeeper. In this latter role, Fred once spent the entire day building a new tee for one of the holes. He knew his turf and took great care to lay it level, fitting the pieces together in a loving jigsaw. At the end of his labours he surveyed his work with that special kind of satisfaction which comes with the knowledge that a job has been well done. With a cheery whistle, Fred went home. That night the Luftwaffe raided the nearby naval base at Portland and one pilot under-clubbed with one of his bombs. It landed dead centre on Fred's new tee and **wiped it from the face of the earth.**

In 1940 golfers were encouraged to carry rifles to deal with parachute invaders.

Ingenious recovery from a water hazard.

The Luftwaffe was not all bad, as witness this story which the late Jack Statter, golf correspondent of *The Sun*, used to recount. One day in occupied Holland a German military car arrived at the Hilversum GC and out stepped a Luftwaffe officer. The officer politely inquired if it would be possible for him to play an occasional round of golf and the Secretary was hardly in a position to decline this request. The German took a bag of clubs out of the car and, with his driver acting as caddie, set forth. The officer became a regular on the course, always playing alone and never once entering the clubhouse.

Then one day a team of German Army engineers arrived at the course and began marking the mighty oak trees for felling to strengthen their 'Atlantic Wall'. When the Luftwaffe golfer saw the marks he got back into his car and drove off. Later that same day he returned with his driver/caddie and together they unloaded from the car a number of notice boards attached to stout posts. These were then posted round every entrance to the course. The German returned to his car and said to the Secretary: 'That should keep them off.'

The signs read: 'Achtung! Es ist verboten . . .' and informed all German military personnel that the golf course was out of bounds to all of them and to all German military vehicles 'by order of the local Commandant of the Gestapo'. The Luftwaffe officer was posted elsewhere shortly afterwards and was never seen again. The trees at Hilversum still stand, a fitting monument to one German who certainly had his priorities right.

Left-hander 'Laddie' Lucas was a noted long-hitter, erratic at times but good enough to be selected for the 1936 British Walker Cup team at Pine Valley, New Jersey. During the war he was a Wing-Commander in a Spitfire squadron and one day was returning from a sortie in France when his plane was hit by enemy fire. With his engine out of action, he glided across the Channel and spied the clubhouse at Prince's on the Kent coast. It was an appropriate landmark since Lucas had been born in the clubhouse and knew every blade of grass on the course. He determined to land his plane on the course but, rather typically, was short on accuracy. He failed to land on any of the fairways on the first nine holes and eventually came to rest in the marshes at the back of the 9th green – **out-of-bounds again!**

FORE!

SHOTS HEARD AROUND THE WORLD

The maxim that every bad shot brings pleasure to someone else is easily reworked to the effect that every good shot brings grief. Epic strokes in championships and tournaments pass into the history of the game with the executioners of those famous shots gaining immortality. Hardly anyone ever remembers the people on the receiving end, so in this chapter we consider the fortunes of both.

Case History No 1. Executioner: Bobby Jones. Victim: Al Watrous.
Exhibit 'A' in this reconstruction of the events surrounding the 1926 Open Championship is a mashie-iron club which now hangs in the clubhouse of Royal Lytham & St Annes. This blunt instrument, the equivalent of a 4-iron today, was used by the distinguished American amateur, Mr Bobby Jones, to bludgeon the

hopes of American professional, Mr Al Watrous. Jones and Watrous were paired together for the final two rounds of this championship which, at that time, were played on the final day.

Following the morning round, Watrous had established a two-stroke lead over Jones but in the afternoon, by the 16th hole, Jones had drawn level. On the 17th hole, or 71st of the championship, Watrous drove safely in the fairway while Jones hooked his tee shot into an area of sandy scrubland. Watrous then struck his second shot onto the green. The precise location of Jones's ball has, even to this day, yet to be confirmed although a plaque has been erected somewhere near the spot. From the evidence obtained, it is sufficient to say that the lie was sandy and presented Jones with an extremely difficult shot. The slightest imperfection in the stroke would send the ball scuttling further forward into more scrubland. Jones executed the stroke perfectly and his ball finished on the green, closer to the flagstick than the ball of Watrous. Watrous is alleged to have commented: 'There goes 100,000 bucks.' He was so upset by this stroke that he three-putted to fall a stroke behind Jones and then three-putted the final hole as well to lose by two shots.

Verdict: Jones found guilty as charged. Sentence: Immortality.

Case History No 2. Executioner: Gene Sarazen. Victim: Craig Wood.

This is a particularly sombre tale concerning the 1935 US Masters. American professional Craig Wood had played quite beautifully to record a total of 282 for the four rounds at Augusta National. He was three strokes ahead of his nearest challenger, Gene Sarazen, who was still out on the course with four holes to play. In order to catch Wood, Sarazen had to birdie three of the last four holes, a tall order by any standards. He neatly side-stepped this problem by holing his second shot with a 4-wood on the par-five 15th hole to make up all three shots in one fell swoop. He then tied with Wood and won the play-off.

Verdict: Sarazen found guilty as charged. Sentence: Immortality.

Case History No 3. Executioner: Lew Worsham. Victim: Chandler Harper.

A clear case of armed robbery. In the 1953 World Championship at the Tam O'Shanter course in Chicago, Lew Worsham, armed with a wedge, holed his second shot of 130 yards to the final green to take the first prize of $25,000 by one stroke from Chandler Harper.

Verdict: Worsham guilty of daylight robbery. Sentence: Vague remembrance

Case History No 4. Executioner: Jack Fleck. Victim: Ben Hogan.

This unprecedented mugging of one of the best players the game has ever seen took place in the 1955 US Open at Olympic Country Club. Although Ben Hogan was still suffering from the effects of his near-fatal road accident some years earlier, he was still a formidable player and it was he who led in the clubhouse after four rounds. Congratulations on a fifth US Open title were showered on Hogan. Out on the course however, an obscure professional from Iowa, Jack Fleck, still had a chance to catch the great man. Fleck came to the final hole needing a birdie three for a 67 and the tie. He struck a 7-iron second shot to within eight feet and calmly rolled the putt home. Next day in the play-off, Fleck held a one-stroke lead after 17 holes. On the 18th tee, Hogan lost his footing on his tee shot and hooked the ball into deep rough, eventually holing out in six. Fleck's solid four gave him the title by three strokes.

Verdict: Guilty as charged. Sentence: Fleck rapidly returned to the obscurity from which he emerged.

Case History No 5. Executioner: Jerry Pate. Victim: John Mahaffey.

In the 1976 US Open at Atlanta Athletic Club, Jerry Pate perpetrated a foul deed on John Mahaffey. The weapon in this instance was a 5-iron which Pate used to hit his second shot to the final hole. The ball carried 190 yards over water and stopped some three feet from the hole. Mahaffey, who had lost a play-off for the same title the year before, then dumped his second shot in the water and didn't even finish second.

Verdict: Guilty of mental aggravation. Sentence: Pate was absolved two years later when, in the 1978 US PGA Championship, he three-putted the final green to fall into a tie with Tom Watson and Mahaffey. Mahaffey won the sudden-death play-off.

Case Histories Nos 6, 7, 8, etc. Executioner: Severiano Ballesteros. Victims: Most current tournament professionals and sundry championship courses.

This is a most unusual case in that the player concerned is still at large. Severiano Ballesteros is an habitual plunderer of the reputations of both players and courses. His first public act in this respect occurred in the 1976 Open Championship at Royal Birkdale when he brazenly chipped his ball between two bunkers on the 72nd hole of the championship. Other similar acts soon followed. In the 1978 Hennessy Cognac Cup match at The Belfry, playing against Nick Faldo, Ballesteros was one up when the two players arrived at the 10th hole. This hole measured 310 yards, turning sharply right to a green protected by water and a tall stand of trees. The conventional way to play the hole is to hit an iron safely down the fairway and then pitch over the water onto the green. This was the route Faldo chose. Ballesteros chose the direct route and struck a towering, fading drive which carried some 284 yards onto the green from where he two-putted for a winning birdie.

In the 1979 Open Championship at Royal Lytham & St Annes, Ballesteros's final round contained numerous wayward drives, the most famous coming at the 16th when he drove underneath some parked cars. He extricated himself from all these trouble spots and won the title, his victim on this occasion being Hale Irwin. In the 1980 US Masters during the second round, Ballesteros hooked his tee shot at the 17th savagely, the ball finishing on the 7th green. He lifted and replaced his ball on the edge of the green and then struck a towering 7-iron over a scoreboard, over some trees and onto the green, holing the resultant fifteen-footer for a birdie. He won the tournament. In the final round of the 1983 US Masters, which he also won, he hit a 4-wood second shot to the long second hole from a hanging lie and settled the ball on the green. The subsequent eagle putt which he holed virtually put paid to his nearest challengers, who included Tom Watson, Craig Stadler and Ray Floyd.

Verdict: Guilty *in absentia*. Sentence: This man is still free and highly dangerous on a golf course. Do not attempt to apprehend but instead observe and take note for you may never see his like again.

A Wentworth marker signals another challenge for Seve "the great escapist".

THE MOST VIOLENT GAME

WORST LIGHTNING

The most infamous incidence of lightning striking famous players occurred in the 1975 Western Open in Chicago when Lee Trevino, Bobby Nichols and Jerry Heard were all struck and taken to hospital. All survived but have subsequently suffered from back trouble with only Trevino maintaining his position among the top players. In spite of the many warnings about the dangers of playing while lightning is in the vicinity, golfers persist in carrying on, or shelter under tall trees, sometimes with fatal consequences. In an unnerving experience, Sam Snead's brother was sheltering under a tree with two companions when the tree was struck. The companions were killed outright while Snead suffered severe burns and later discovered that both the zip on his trousers and his nylon socks had melted.

NASTIEST THREATS

As if clinging onto a single-stroke lead in the closing stages of a major championship wasn't pressure enough, Hubert Green had to contend with a death threat during the final round of the 1977 US Open at Southern Hills. As he walked off the 14th green, officials informed Green that they had received a phone call threatening his life and asked him if he wanted to come off the course. Green declined and went on to win the title by one stroke.

In the 1951 St Paul Open, Lloyd Mangrum held a comfortable lead going into the final round. Prior to the start of that round he received a 'phone call telling him that if he didn't 'throw' the tournament, Mrs Mangrum was soon going to be a widow. Apparently, some big money was riding on the outcome of the tournament but Mangrum, who had the looks of a Mississippi gambler and also won two purple hearts in the Second World War, was unmoved by the threat and, accompanied by a police guard, won the tournament. He died in 1973 of natural causes.

MOST VIOLENT FOUR-BALL

At the North West Park GC, Washington in 1975, fighting broke out between members of two four-ball games. One group claimed the other was holding them up, the other group claimed the group behind had driven into them. Tempers flared, clubs were raised in anger resulting in serious injuries, including a fractured skull. The police were called and a court case followed.

ULTIMATE PENALTY

In 1972 at the Delaware Park GC, Buffalo, New York State, John Moseley stepped onto the first tee and was challenged by a guard about his green fee. A fight developed, a shot was fired and Moseley, a bullet in his chest, died on the way to hospital. His wife was awarded $131,250 in damages. The guard was sentenced to $7\frac{1}{2}$ years imprisonment for manslaughter.

BEST PROFESSIONAL FISTICUFFS

During one of his infrequent trips to America, the fiery little Australian golfer Norman von Nida found himself partnering American Ryder Cup player Henry Ransom in the 1948 Lower Rio Grande Open. On one hole, Ransom went to knock in a short putt with one hand and missed. He later insisted he had taken two putts but, at the end of the round, von Nida refused to concur. A fight developed in which von Nida was punched by the American and a local sheriff had to pull them apart. Ransom was later disqualified and banned for three months.

Another piece of aggro occurred in the 1968 Agfa-Gevaert tournament at Stoke Poges involving the late Harry Weetman and 'Himself', Irishman Christy O'Connor. A long and emotional occupancy of the bar ended when Weetman punched O'Connor in response to an alleged remark concerning the lady captain of the club. The next day, neither player could remember the incident although O'Connor played the remainder of the tournament wearing dark glasses in weather conditions which were not all that bright. Both players were fined £50.

MOST BALANCED ROBBERY VICTIM

American touring professional Scott Hoch was looking forward to a successful season when he and his wife booked into a motel for the 1982 Tucson Open. During the night, thieves broke into his room, tied up Hoch and his wife and removed $4,500 from the family coffers. In view of this experience, Hoch played commendably well in the event, finishing in a tie for 15th place to win, you've guessed it, $4,500.

MOST DAMAGED SPECTATORS

Charles Smillie was taking an afternoon stroll with his son on a public footpath adjoining the Woburn Golf & Country Club during the final round of the 1981 Dunlop Masters. He paused to watch some of the action on the other side of the fence but his dallying caused him to lose five of his teeth, removed by an errant tee shot struck by the powerful Scot, Sam Torrance. Mr Smillie brought an action for damages against the club which Woburn defended by claiming that he was using the path to watch the tournament, thereby avoiding payment of the entry fee. The judge ruled against Woburn and awarded the plaintiff £10,000 on the grounds that the club had failed to take reasonable steps to warn people of the potential danger.

Shortly after this verdict at the High Court in London, the Dublin Circuit Civil Court ordered that £824 be paid to a spectator at the 1982 Carrolls Irish Open who caught his foot in a hole on the course and tore the ligaments in his leg. These sums for damages were easily exceeded in the case of a lady who was watching the Western Open in Chicago in 1983. She was struck by a golf ball, lost the sight of one eye and received $448,380 in compensation.

MOST VOLATILE RESPONSE

In the Italian Open one year, an Italian player three-putted a green much to the anguish of himself and also a watching compatriot. The spectator rushed across the green and punched the player on the nose.

HOTTEST DISPUTE

As a result of an incident at a California course in 1978, golfer Jim Brown was convicted of beating and choking an opponent in a dispute over where a ball should have been placed on the green.

FALSEST ALARM

The ambulance crew responded in minutes to a call from the Point Grey GC in Vancouver following a report that a golfer had suffered a heart attack. Justice J. M. Coady, aged 95 and a likely candidate for such a stricture, had been spotted resting in a golf buggy. A passing golfer had asked him what the problem was and thought the Judge replied: 'Heart failure.' He didn't. Justice Coady's buggy had broken down and he actually said:'Cart failure'.

OLDEST FIGHT-BACK

Monsignor Vincent O'Leary, aged 72, Dr W. Millard (87) and Jim Breytspraak (66) were on the 8th green of the Overland Park GC in Memphis when a man emerged from the bushes and demanded their wallets. The golfers refused to part with their money and a scuffle developed, the mugger wrestling Dr Millard to the ground. Monsignor O'Leary, club in hand, approached the two combatants. With Divine Guidance on his side, the priest maintained a steady head and accelerated the club accurately on the villain's skull. The would-be robber staggered off empty-handed.

MOST THREATENING WEAPONS

Customs officials at Heathrow Airport were understandably nervous when they spotted a box labelled 'Assault with a deadly weapon'. They gingerly opened the box which was found to contain nothing more offensive than advertising literature for Greenirons, an American golf club manufacturer. The phrase was their advertising slogan.

MOST LUCRATIVE SIDELINE

Richard Meissner did not win a cent of prize-money in the 26 US Tour events he entered in 1977 and 1978. It turned out that he had an alternative source of income – bank robbing. Meissner was arrested in 1978 and found guilty of robbing banks in Virginia and Maryland to the tune of $100,000 from 19 hold-ups. He was sentenced to a prison term of up to twenty-five years.

MOST VIOLENT COUP DURING A GOLF TOURNAMENT

When John Cook won the 1969 English Amateur Championship, a professional career beckoned. The opportunity to travel to faraway places with strange sounding names took Cook to Morocco for the 1971 Trophee Hassan. This tournament is patronized by King Hassan of Morocco, an avid golfer, and is a sumptuous event. The revels that year centred on the King's birthday and a celebration party at the palace in Rabat was in full swing when rebels brought the proceedings to a sudden end by breaking in and demanding that the King give up his throne. Armed with machine-guns, the insurgents took Cook and many others as hostages and began a systematic series of executions. Over 200 people were shot before the King surrendered, with Cook narrowly escaping the firing squad. The King eventually regained control and the Trophee Hassan continues as a tournament. On the other hand, Cook, not surprisingly, forsook the professional ranks and now runs a pub in a more peaceful resort in Cornwall.

ACES HIGH AND LOW

A hole-in-one is the ultimate stroke in golf, its perfection cannot be beaten and its perpetrator can bask in its glow forever. The odds against achieving this feat are astonishingly high, emerging roughly as follows: male professional or top amateur, 3,708 to 1; female professional or top lady amateur, 4,658 to 1; average golfer, 42,952 to 1. In 1951 a competition was held in New York when 1,409 players who had done a hole-in-one played over several days at short holes on three local courses. Each player was allowed five shots, giving an aggregate of 7,045 attempts. No-one holed-in-one. In spite of these enormous odds, golfers throughout the world have achieved practically every conceivable record that is possible with the ultimate stroke.

Even amidst the joy engendered by the feat, **fate still lurks with the loaded glove,** as in the case of the New Zealand golfer who holed-in-one at the 6th and, while walking to the next tee with a spring in his step, was knocked unconscious by a ball driven from the nearby 8th tee. Take heed also from the experience of Charles Coody in the 1972 US Masters. As defending champion, Coody had every reason to believe that the Georgia sunshine would continue to shine exlusively on him when, in the first round, he holed-in-one at the 6th. At the next hole he was suddenly enveloped in a deep pall of gloom. The hole measures just 365 yards and is one of the shortest par fours on the course. Coody holed out in seven. Consider too the circumstances concerning a certain Dr Tucker in 1936 at a course in New Orleans. The good doctor put his name down for a hole-in-one competition. He then repaired to the competition hole, put down a ball and holed-in-one. He rushed back to the clubhouse to impart his good tidings. When he got there he found that the competition was not due to begin for another two weeks.

In the 1974 Penfold Tournament at Worthing, professional Peter Wilcock holed-in-one at the 5th to win a prize of a car, worth £2,000. He achieved his ace in the second round but since the prize was on offer throughout the tournament, Wilcock took the precaution of insuring against having to share the spoils of his good fortune with another professional. It was a wise move for, in the very next round, another hole-in-one was achieved. The only slight drawback was that it was by the same player.

At Rochford GC, Essex, one Sunday morning a player said he had dreamed he had done the 10th hole in one. His companions were scornful and commented on his over-indulgence the night before. Some sizeable bets were struck and when the player arrived at the 10th, a good crowd had gathered. To everyone's amazement, the player holed-in-one and the hole is still known as **'The Dream Hole'**.

John Hudson celebrates his two consecutive holes-in-one in the 1971 Martini International at Royal Norwich.

Two golfers approached the 187-yard 12th hole of the Box Valley GC in Wisconsin. The sun was low and the first player hit his 3-wood towards the green into the glare. The second player followed suit with a 4-wood. On reaching the green they found one ball in the hole, but since both of them were playing with the same type and numbered ball, they do not know to this day who had the hole-in-one.

It should never be forgotten that a hole-in-one is only one stroke in a round and therefore has exactly the same value as a one-inch putt or a 250-yard drive. This fact may have escaped Eric Fiddian while playing in the 36-hole final of the 1933 Irish Open at Royal County Down. In the morning round, Fiddian holed-in-one at the 7th and then repeated the feat at the 14th in the afternoon. His opponent, Jack McLean, was obviously unmoved by these flamboyant strokes and defeated Fiddian by 3 and 2.

On occasions, a hole-in-one has no value whatsoever, as in the case of professional Stuart Brown who, while playing in the 1980 Kenya Open, hooked his tee shot to the short 2nd hole at the Muthaiga GC into some bushes. Brown followed the correct procedure and announced he was playing a provisional ball. He then hit his provisional ball straight into the hole. Unfortunately for him, his original ball was found and he eventually holed out in four. When play was over for the day, Brown found he had missed the 36-hole cut by one stroke. Similar devaluation was experienced by Robert Saalfield playing the 195-yard 7th at the Savannah GC, Georgia. Saalfield hit his first two tee shots out-of-bounds and then **holed out with his third attempt for a five-in-one.**

As mentioned earlier in this chapter, in order to get your hole-in-one in the record books, you have to do something exceptional. Perhaps you might feel that your total of say five holes-in-one in a lifetime is worthy of inclusion. Forget it. Amateur Norman Manley of Long Beach, California is the current leader with 47 aces so far in his life. Manley also achieved the incredible feat of successive holes-in-one at two par-four holes, the history-making strokes occurring at the 330-yard 7th and the 290-yard 8th of the Del Valle Country Club, California, in September 1964. The feat of scoring successive holes-in-one in a full professional tournament has been achieved only once. In the 1971 Martini International at Royal Norwich, British professional John Hudson holed-in-one with a 4-iron at the 190-yard 11th and after a twenty-minute wait on the next tee, holed out again with a driver on the downhill 311-yard 12th; on this occasion the ball ran through the players still putting on the green.

In the 1974 Eastern Counties Foursomes at Hunstanton, Bob Taylor, a member of the Leicestershire team, set a unique record by holing-in-one at the same hole, the 16th, on three successive days. The first occurred in practice with a 1-iron and the other two in competition, both with a 6-iron. These most repetitive aces were almost equalled by John Murphy who holed his tee shot at the 175-yard 5th hole at the Wil-Mar GC, Raleigh, North Carolina. Since he was playing alone, his ace was unofficial, so after the round he took the assistant greenkeeper out with him to the same hole, put down a ball and repeated the feat.

Another record in this department was set by 26-year-old Scott Palmer of San Diego in 1983, when he became the first player to score a **hole-in-one on four consecutive days.** He recorded his feat at the Balboa Park

Municipal Course in his home town by respectively holing out with his driver on the 260-yard 6th on day one, a 5-iron at the 198-yard 8th on day two, a wedge at the 150-yard 1st on day three and finally a 6-iron at the 8th again. It should be stated that this record was achieved on a nine-hole course with four par three holes, thus affording more possibilities than usual.

One of the most enduring world records is that held by Robert Mitera who claimed the **longest hole-in-one** when he holed his tee shot on the 447-yard 10th at the aptly named Miracle Hill GC in Omaha. The ground sloped sharply downhill and he was aided by a strong following wind.

In 1981 at Beamish GC in Co Durham, seventeen-year-old Stephen Wightman decided, for a laugh, to play the 174-yard 4th using his putter from the tee. The ball rocketed off the putter, never rising above waist height, landed on the green and ran into the hole.

When the mandarins at Baltusrol, New Jersey wanted to toughen up their course for the 1954 US Open, they brought in the eminent architect Robert Trent Jones. At the end of the work, the committee protested that Jones had made the course too tough, in particular the short 4th hole which had to be played across water to a narrow green protected by bunkers at the back. Jones disagreed with the officials and took them out to the hole to test it out. The officials all hit their shots and then it was Jones's turn. His shot flew towards the green, pitched and rolled gently into the hole.

'As you can see, gentlemen,' said Jones, 'this hole is not too tough.'

The **earliest recorded ace** occurred in the Open Championship of 1868, when Young Tom Morris, in the first of his four consecutive victories in the event, holed-in-one at the 145-yard 8th at Prestwick.

Most hole-in-one records are held by men but one record held by Nila Morrison of Michigan is unlikely to be beaten by a man. In 1967, Mrs Morrison had a hole-in-one two days before she gave birth to a son. This record has not been seriously challenged since, although in 1982 Kitty Peck holed-in-one at the Recreation GC in California two weeks before she gave birth to her son.

Swiss golfer Otto Bucher became the **oldest player to hole-in-one** when, at the age of 99 in January 1985, he aced the 130-yard 13th with a 5-iron on La Manga's South Course. This beat the previous record held jointly by three American striplings who were aged only 93 at the time of their achievement.

Keep trying, everyone!

PLEASE LADY, DON'T GET TOO EXCITED

ACKNOWLEDGMENTS

The publishers would like to acknowledge with thanks the following sources which supplied some of the stories around which this book has been developed:

The Benson & Hedges *Golfer's Handbook;* the PGA European Tour; the Association of Golf Writers; *The Halford Hewitt: A Festival of Foursomes* by Peter Ryde; *Seve: The Young Champion* by Dudley Doust; and various other magazines and newspapers.

The publishers would also like to thank the following sources for their help in providing illustrations:

Peter Blackbrow/*Golf Illustrated*
Dave Cannon/*Allsport Photographic*
Peter Dazeley
Keith Hailey
Ian Joy
Illustrated London News Picture Library
Bert Neale/*Action Photos*
The Photosource
Popperfoto
Rex Features
Phil Sheldon
S & G Press Agency